FROM MONK TO MODERNITY

With Best Wishes

Dominic Kirkham

24 July 2015

Dedication

To the memory of George Tyrrell,

a victim of modernity

and to

Celine and all the friends

who have made my life possible.

From Monk to Modernity

The Challenge of Modern Thinking

Dominic Kirkham

SOF

Sea of Faith Network

First published on 24th July 2015 by SOF
Sea of Faith Network
28 Frederick Road,
Birmingham B15 1JN
www.sofn.org.uk
© copyright Dominic Kirkham 2015
The front cover image is of Dante and Virgil in the Dark Wood,
one of William Blake's illustrations to Dante's *Divine Comedy*.
Image in the public domain.
Designed and typeset in-house mainly in 11 point Garamond.
Printed in England by imprint.co.uk/digital

ISBN: 978-0-9523930-3-0

British Library cataloguing in publication data:
A catalogue record for this book is available from the British Library.

CONTENTS

III. HERE AND NOW

FOREWORD

This is a book of personal reflections in the form of essays. They gravitate around one central issue: what it means to be modern. Though each chapter is autonomous, together they explore different aspects of this issue in the search for how we have become modern and its implications.

The preface is intended to provide a context of why this is of concern to me, the writer, and how the chapters have come to be written. This is something of a personal odyssey, which now spans a lifetime of over six decades and is still ongoing. The presumption of the book is that this is of more than personal interest because the subject affects everyone; my personal journey will no doubt reflect that of many others.

Modernity is quite an ambiguous if not vacuous word, which can be used to cover almost anything. It is a word often associated with a Western way of life, also an ambiguous and sometimes polemical concept. For reasons that will become apparent, my particular interest is in its religious and epistemic aspects.

Though my use of the word 'modernity' is general and embrace a summary description of it, at least in its philosophical sense, given by the sociologist and philosopher Jürgen Habermas is useful:

> The project of modernity formulated in the eighteenth century by the philosophers of the Enlightenment consisted in their efforts to develop objective science, universal morality and law, and art, according to their inner logic. At the same time, this project intended to release the cognitive potentials of each of these domains from their esoteric forms.

There is no specific purpose or thesis behind these reflections, no secret intent or sub-text. They are explorations which surf the minds of many writers and thinkers from many times and places on many different subjects; they seek to identify changes in human understanding that have taken place over many millennia. They draw on a collective and ecumenical endeavour which I hope will, in the end, give a deeper insight into a life which is modern.

I would like to thank the editor of *Sofia* magazine, Dinah Livingstone, for providing the inspiration for this book and suggesting its title, as well as arranging all the publication details. Thanks also go to the trustees of SOF (Sea of Faith) Network who have made its publication possible.

Dominic Kirkham

PREFACE

A Personal Journey from Monasticism to Modernity

I write as a victim. – ah! how the world loves a victim – though not a victim in the ordinary sense; rather as a victim to modernity. But, then, as change is forced upon us and unfortunate adaptations have to be made, aren't we all, to some extent, victims of modernity?

But what is modernity and when did it begin? Humans have always liked to define their place in the world by so-called 'threshold' events, such as the beginning of a dynasty, or B.C and A.D. (before and after Christ) or A.H. (after the Hejira), or perhaps even the French Revolution, when the modern world has often been said to begin. Now we are told by scientists that we have reached a new stage in planetary history and live in a new geological era: the *anthropocene* or human epoch. Just as scholarly divines once assured us that the world began on 23 October 4004 BC at 9am – for precision has always been a central part of human progress – scientists now tell us this new epoch began on 16th July 1945 at 5:29:21 (+/- 2 seconds). On that day and time, precisely, the first nuclear explosion took place at Alamogordo in New Mexico: humans had become a force of geological proportions with the power to leave an indelible mark on the Earth. Some even said man had become God, the creator and destroyer of worlds (this nuclear event was codenamed 'Trinity' – the title of the Christian Godhead). Or was this simply hubris?

Another date for the starting of our modern age has been given as the 13th September 1830.[1] On that day, just before 3 pm on a drizzly afternoon, a steam locomotive pulled into Manchester's new Liverpool Street Station, having completed the world's first passenger trip on the opening of the world's first public railway line. What was special about this event was not just that this was the first train service but that it was pulled by a machine which transformed the world and

---

1. S. & D. Duggan, *The Day the World Took Off: The Roots of the Industrial Revolution* (Channel 4 Books, 2000).

epitomised the new age of steam power. It was steam power which had already made possible the cotton mills of Manchester, the new phenomenon of their time; they were also notorious for reasons Fredrick Engels would shortly make clear in his seminal work on the *Condition of The Working Class*, which would help to substantiate the most potent ideology of modernity, communism. This was the first industrialised city and it was steam power that began the processes of industrialisation which would transform the world, create the possibility of globalisation and herald modernity.

Though these issues may be vast, the specific dates and events associated with them have shaped my life, like those of so many others, in very personal ways. I always remember the 16th July because it is my birthday: I was born in Manchester at the beginning of this new anthropocene epoch, on the very threshold of the age in which we all now live. My grandfathers played a small role in expanding the 'empire of steam', one as the Chief Engineer of the Bengal or East India Railways and the other as a cotton merchant in the city. Their ancestral presence has shaped my life in ways that still surprise me, particularly my maternal grandfather, who became a convert to the newly invigorated ultramontane Roman Catholicism of the mid-nineteenth century. I grew up in Manchester, the city which proudly claimed to be a workshop of the world and where the atom was first split. Later, in mid-life I lived as a priest for fifteen years in a parish dominated by one of the greatest of the few surviving mills in Manchester, the Victoria Mill of Miles Platting. It is a mill I helped to save for posterity, together with the central historic complex of cotton mills in Ancoats (now a UNESCO World Heritage site). It was in the shadow of these mills that I sought to persuade government ministers to support our community regeneration schemes and around which I accompanied Prince Charles. This is all part of the modern world which has also been very much a part of my life.

But what does it mean to be modern? How did we get to be 'modern' and perhaps more importantly, what will the future hold for us? These are questions that have long pre-occupied me and which I attempt to address in this book. It is a book which, like the modern age, has disturbing undertones. The book cover, with its painting by Blake, is not accidental. It shows a scene from the life of the Italian poet, Dante, who wrote that on being expelled from the city of

Florence in 1302, 'in the middle of the pathway of our life I found myself in a dark wood where the right way was lost.' This also is our predicament today, not only as individuals but as a species, as we wander into what has been called the penumbra of the Enlightenment. It is into 'the dark wood' of modernity that this book, like my life, leads.

The modern world has been led from the hope of Enlightenment – with its dream of reason – to a place of increasing darkness. In fact this seemed implicit almost from the outset. It was reflected in the apocalyptic vision of 'dark satanic mills' of the visionary William Blake: mills, which not only ground out goods and ground down people, but mills of the mind which dreamed up new 'demonic' plans. And it was indeed an apocalyptic age for, in one of the many paradoxes of modernity, the 'great acceleration' of progress has led us to the brink of catastrophe. It was at this point of our history that the natural 'footprint' of Britain began to exceed its sustainable carrying capacity and that carbon emissions began to escalate remorselessly. The carbon emissions of those belching mills now linger over the planet in gathering plumes threatening a climate change which could end life on this planet as we know it. In fact such a transformation of life is already happening with the greatest collapse of species and ecosystems since life emerged from the sea to colonise the land 300 million years ago. This has been called 'the sixth extinction' – a humanly induced biological collapse after five such previous geological events – which also has been seen as the harbinger of a new age, alternatively called (by the dystopian prophet and philosopher John Gray) the Eremozoic, the era of solitude, in which little remains on Earth, perhaps not even mankind itself.

Not only has our species threatened the destruction of all other species in this anthropocene age, it threatens itself. Its utopian dreams, exponential growth and insatiable consumption require more than one Earth – in fact it has been estimated we already need two and half Earths to carry on living in the way we do. The fantasy entity necessary to support human ambition has even been given a name (by environmentalist Bill McKibben), 'Eaarth' – a bigger Earth, which we do not have even though people live as if we do. Meanwhile, on the Earth we do have, as well as destroying other species, we have been busy destroying our own. New words have appeared for new events: 'holocaust', 'ethnic cleansing', 'genocide', in which whole peoples and cultural groups have been threatened with extinction. World War and the totalitarian ideologies of modernity have seen civilised people reduced to foraging as hunter-gatherers in the forests of Europe whilst in Asia, as in the killing fields of Cambodia, whole societies have been reduced to a new Stone Age. Welcome to modernity!

Modernity has its problems and challenges for traditional ways and modes of thought. This is particularly true for religion and the religiously minded. As one who was brought up a Roman Catholic, received all my education in Catholic institutes, becoming a teacher and then – after seemingly interminable years at a seminary – being ordained as a priest, and spending nearly thirty years in a religious order, the challenge of new ways of thinking, and the changes that were introduced into the church as a result, have been a particular concern and constant undercurrent.

For much of the twentieth century the ultimate threat to the Catholic Church was seen to be 'modernism', declared to be, by Pope Pius X in 1907, the 'synthesis of all heresies'. It was deemed all the more pernicious for being insidious, difficult to identify and pin down, not only in what it said but the way it said it, always, as the famous Benedictine Abbot Vonier once wrote, referring everything to 'experience', as if this were the highest court of appeal and final justification. Ironically, in so far as 'isms' – those great nebulous systems of thought – are a hallmark of modernity and the way in which it expresses itself, Pope Pius was showing himself also to be very modern. The social theologian Gregory Baum captured this irony in his perceptive comment, 'Whenever a religion vehemently rejects a modern society, it integrates certain elements of modernity into the new formed orthodoxy.' We see this happening currently among radical Islamists, with their hatred of modernity and obsession with tradition but addiction to modern technology. Regardless of this, the pope went on to denounce anyone suspected of compromising the traditional deposit of faith (as he saw it) with modern ways of thinking. The effect of such a pronouncement was to create something akin to a modern witch-hunt – very much after the manner of McCarthyism in America of the 1950s – which grew to frightening proportions, ruining many lives and careers.

One early and famous casualty of the 'war on modernism' in this country was the prominent Jesuit theologian and popular writer, George Tyrrell. Now largely a forgotten figure, he sought to re-appraise traditional belief in the light of the modern world and modern thinking. His efforts led to his excommunication (never formalised) from the church, though he vigorously defended himself and decried the church for its 'medievalism'. His career terminated, he continued to pursue his thoughts until an early death and he was buried as an apostate in an Anglican churchyard in the remote Sussex village of Storrington. It is interesting to speculate what he might have thought of the recent criticism of the Vatican curia by the present Pope Francis, that it is suffering from 'spiritual Alzheimer's' – a pithy remark that succinctly expresses the central critique of Tyrrell's writings.

I mention all this because, by coincidence, the monastic cell of the religious order which I joined as a young man and where I lived for twelve years, overlooked this churchyard and his grave.[2] Occasionally visitors would come in search of it and for some insight into his background. I learnt that he had been treated kindly by the Prior of the monastery – himself and his community recent refugees from Provence in the bitter conflict with modernity then raging in the Third French Republic – and that he would spend long hours in thoughtful prayer in the monastery church. For a time he lived in the monastery. Sometimes, on a summer's evening I would sit among the wild flowers of the glebe meadow that adjoined the monastery and graveyard, with its isolated plot surrounded by an evergreen laurel hedge, and as the sun set, would reflect on lives long past, of destinies frustrated and dreams dashed.[3]

---

2. Strictly speaking the Premonstratensian Order to which I belonged were Canons Regular, i.e. they followed the rule of St Augustine rather than St. Benedict. It was founded in 1121 at Prémontré, in the forests of northern France, by Norbert of Xanten as a new – 'modern' – form of radical community of shared life for men and women.

3. For an appreciation of George Tyrrell's life and thinking Ellen Leonard's *George Tyrrell and the Catholic Tradition* (Darton, Longman and Todd, 1982) cannot be bettered. I remember showing her around the monastery library when she was researching for her book; of particular interest was the caged section where works on the Index of Forbidden Books were once locked away: more latterly this was used to store the snooker equipment.

As my own career unfolded I too became more and more challenged by modernity and the church's response to it. The Vatican
Council of the 1960s had been a watershed moment for the church.
Pope John XXIII was the first pope to stop deploring the modern
world and speak positively of its achievements; he wanted to 'throw
open the windows', let in fresh air and break out of what had become
a stifling, schizoid institution – one that moved in a world which had
become completely alien to its way of thinking. Despite its univer-
salist pretensions, the Roman Catholic Church was, as the name
implies, the product of a distinctive European cultural tradition. Pope
John's council was the first to move beyond token gestures and become a global event in its attempt to engage with the whole world
and create a truly global – as distinct from Eurocentric – church. Its
leitmotif would be, how to read 'the signs of the times'.

A central issue was the understanding of authority. It was really
quite simple. For Catholics the authority of the clergy was absolute,
and unconditional obedience expected: there was a teaching *ecclesia
docens* and a passive *ecclesia discerns:* an official *magisterium* which was
infallible and inerrant, and then the laity who just did as they were
told (or were supposed to). Even the right of conscience to dissent
had really no status for, in the words of the well-known phrase, error
has no rights. Sometimes issues might arise that caused controversy
– the treatment of Jews or Galileo, or the Chinese Rites, spring to
mind – but potential criticism of the church could always be deflected
by blaming deviant individuals or defective procedures. The church,
in essence, was always pristine and perfect.

This depiction of the church, focused on an over-centralised
hierarchy which expected an entirely 'docile' laity, is what Tyrrell had
called the 'Vatican heresy' and it had been at the centre of his dispute
with the church authorities. He thought that it did not reflect the true
nature of the church in its origins and he contrasted this hierarchical
elitism with the earlier inclusive view, in which the seat of authority
was the church as a whole: the *consensus fidelium* or community of the
faithful. These differing views of the seat of power mirrored the wider
tensions in the modern secular world, with the emergence of
democratic and liberal ideals after the French Revolution, struggling
to assert 'the will of the people'. In 1864 Pope Pius IX denounced
this trend in his *Syllabus of Errors*.

It was the ferment of the new thinking and ideas associated with the Vatican Council, as it attempted to break away from the past and the great sense of excitement they generated that prompted me to take a greater involvement in the life of the church. Having begun a career as a teacher (of history), I felt called to move on and join a religious order. At this time, in the vibrancy of the 1960s, there was a feeling which was also reflected in the excitement that the church was at last responding to 'the signs of the times' in a positive way: as one up-coming theologian named Joseph Ratzinger put it, 'Something of the Kennedy era pervaded the Council, something of the naïve optimism of the concept of the great society.' This could be seen in the way Pope John had designated that his council would be a 'pastoral council', which by its very nature would be an open affair with many officially invited 'observers'. It was a sign of the desire to move on beyond the old confrontational and centralised church to a more fruitful and embracive conversation with the modern world. New concepts began to emerge such as 'collegiality', 'subsidiarity' and 'inculturation', which emphasised the collective nature of the church and the decentralising of power; others such as 'ecumenism' and 'conscientisation' were difficult to pronounce, let alone comprehend. People wondered what it all meant: challenging times indeed!

The changes proved traumatic and destabilising for many. It can be debated whether this was a direct consequence of Vatican II or, as the theologian Yves Congar argued, it was an aspect of the 'socio-cultural mutation (of modernity) whose amplitude, radicality, rapidity, and global character have no equivalent in any other period of history'. For a time it felt as if the lid had blown off a pressure cooker with ensuing confusion. Ultimately, it led to a conservative reaction which gathered pace in the neo-orthodox pontificate of John Paul II. Despite his enduring popularity, his approach to the modern world was more confrontational. He was a product of a country in the grip of a bitter ideological struggle then raging in Eastern Europe with a totalitarian Soviet system, the epicentre of the so called Cold War. In this clash of Titans the Polish church, with its overwhelming popular support, had been able to confront its atheist adversary precisely because of its formidable discipline, monolithic structure and central-ised authority. Ironically, these were the very characteristics that had typified the pre-conciliar church in its struggle with modernism, which Pope John had tried to move beyond.[4]

It was at this time that a chance came for me to tour Poland, visiting several famous monasteries and experiencing at first hand the persecution of the church under a modern ideological system – though I had previously visited Russia as a student on a cultural exchange. I even had an opportunity to interview the leader of the resistance or Solidarity movement, Lech Walesa. To be caught up in such a tide of popular religious fervour and defiance in the face of an overbearing tyranny was unlike anything I had experienced. It was exhilarating and the subsequent election of a Polish pope seemed to confirm a momentous triumph.

The problem was that Pope John Paul II's populism disguised an underlying 'monarchialism' quite at variance with the understanding of the Vatican Council. Now the engagement with modernity, as it manifested itself in the secular West, took on once more the attributes not of Pope John's conversation but of the previous spirit of outright confrontation, as the new pope strove to restore internal discipline to the church. Just as in Tyrrell's time, when the church had condemned 'Americanism' and Christian Democracy, so now it condemned the Liberation movement in South America. The attempt to refocus the church on the local 'base communities' was seen as a direct challenge to the authority of the Vatican, which resolutely set about crushing it.[5] The need for a new sense of 'being the church' in the modern

---

4. The question of how exactly John Paul II understood the Vatican Council is crucial to understanding subsequent events. A study of his reporting of the council to the Polish church in *Sources of Renewal* is revealing for what he omitted or misrepresented, which one Vatican commentator called 'chilling' (Peter Hebblethwaite, *Introducing John Paul II* (Collins, 1982, p.64). Another Polish commentator, Halina Bortnowska, noted the work gave the surreal impression that there had been no debate, leaving 'a feeling of great abstractness and remoteness'. See also M. Faggioli, *Vatican II: The Battle for Meaning* (Paulist Press, 2012).

5. The base communities of the poor in the slums of the great cities of Latin America were seen not only as a challenge to the church but also to the state (at the time mainly dictatorships) and denounced as communist. As one of its figureheads, Bishop Hélder Câmara, famously said: 'I helped the poor and they called me a saint. I asked why they were poor and they called me a communist.' The Vatican sided with the vicious right-wing dictatorships in crushing the movement, as in Argentina, Chile and El Salvador, where Archbishop Oscar

world was gradually discarded in favour of the traditional centralised power structure. It was, as the novelist Giuseppe Lampedusa had once cryptically observed of the *Risorgimento* (the Italian reunification movement), as if everything had changed only to remain the same.

These developments began to disturb me but it was at this time of conflicting currents and emotions that I was moved from the monastery in the Sussex countryside to an inner city parish in Manchester, where I would serve for fifteen years. By coincidence it was not far from my home and the place where an aunt had taught as a nun many years before. It was a rather dramatic change, from a rural idyll to an encounter with the challenges of modern urban living at the bottom of the social ladder in a notoriously deprived area: according to the lurid headlines of the local paper at the time it was 'A Nightmare in a City of Shame'.[6] As a result of the social needs, I became more and more involved in regeneration schemes, together with the other churches in the area. This was the time of the major Anglican reassessment of parochial life, *Faith in the City* (1985), which added impetus to our endeavours. Through our community initiatives, of which I was the secretary, the headlines were gradually reversed, particularly after winning The Times/Touche-Ross 'Award for Business in the Community', which was presented by Prince Charles on a visit to the parish. It also earned invitations for parishioners to St. James's Palace and even tea on the lawns of Buckingham Palace.

Whilst one could make progress with community projects, which I helped to initiate, it was more difficult to change vestigial parochial attitudes that regarded the church as something of a sacramental machine running on the side-lines of life. Old traditions lingered on but often with little more than a marginal relevance. It was also difficult for people to understand the new, ecumenical parish social

---

Romero was shot during Mass in 1980. Like the USA under President Reagan, the church under John Paul II was generally supportive of these philo-fascist regimes in the interests of security and stability, though this 'neo-Augustinian' alliance of throne and altar was something that the Council had sought to move beyond.

6. The headline that appeared in the *Manchester Evening News* referred not only to high levels of crime and unemployment but to some of the worst health statistics in the country.

schemes in the context of traditional ways. Sometimes new developments might cause a ripple of concern, such as the reception of a group of disaffected Anglicans into the church who were opposed to the ordination of women. Why, some wondered, was this such a taboo subject – forbidden even to be discussed – and why was it that married Anglican clergy could be admitted but not marriage for Catholic clergy? People murmured, but there were no satisfactory answers. For some there was a sense of aggrievement that problems in the church had arisen because of unnecessary change and their resolution lay in a return to traditional certainties.

In the end, with the declining attendance rates and continued re-housing schemes in the area, which uprooted many of the parishioners, the parish ceased to be viable. The school was closed and demolished and plans were made for the Order to vacate the parish and return it to the diocese. This subsequently happened and the grand basilica and parish centre would in time become an Asian Banqueting Suite. A sign of the times indeed!

More disturbing for me was the increasingly reactionary nature of the church under the direction of Pope John Paul. Renewal was gradually but systematically being replaced by a similar sounding but subtly different counterfeit: a repackaging of the past. Challenging new concepts, such as the description of the church as 'the People of God', were 'entombed' and just disappeared from official use, whilst others, such as 'collegiality', were 'reinterpreted' so as to check their implicit challenge to central authority. Theologians who pursued lines of thought opened up by the Council, such as the Sri Lankan Tissa Balasuriya writing on inculturation, were censored. The threat of excommunication returned once more and the exploration of new possibilities was scotched; pastiche was everything, nothing quite as it seemed. The dialogue with the world envisaged by the Council subtly changed from an open ended conversation furthering new understanding to a manipulative engagement. Bizarrely, Buddhism was condemned for its 'autoeroticism' – which one wit (the local Dean) translated as 'love of cars'!

Now it seemed too much deliberation was deemed destabilising, so certain 'principles of interpretation' were enforced, as in the famous *Ratzinger Report* of 1985, in which it was denied that compromises had been made in conciliar discussions or that 'it would be necessary to go courageously beyond the texts' – as John XXIII had anticipated. Numerous proclamations (such as encyclical letters), intended as clear statements of 'the truth', subtly transformed the exploratory intentions of the Council for a pilgrim church and one such document, ostentatiously entitled 'The Splendour of Truth' (*Veritatis Splendor*), was even described by an Anglican bishop as 'spiritual Stalinism'. This was followed by reintroducing a new form of Pius X's 'Anti-Modernist Oath' for clergy to ensure doctrinal conformity. As in the Polish church of the communist era, there would be no dissent.

In the end I found that as a priest and official witness to the church I could no longer go along with this charade; it contradicted everything I had come to think about the church so, after fifty years of life in the church and nearly thirty in a religious order, I left. At the time it was quite difficult to have a balanced perspective of oneself or one's thoughts though, needless to say, such decisions are not taken lightly. But looking back now, some twenty years on, I am not sure any decision was taken at all. Rather, it was a pragmatic reaction to a conjunction of circumstances which has so often typified my life. There was no 'Martin Luther moment', nothing dramatic or done in high dudgeon but quietly through the back door, literally: I remember the latch clicking as I walked away with a finality as when Adam walked out of Eden, and I just returned home to look after my aging father.

As a means of survival I was able to find part time employment in one of the community enterprises I had helped to start – a security and ironwork company – and subsequently I found more substantial employment at a Home Improvement Agency providing services for older people, doing household repairs and running DIY courses. Here I could make full use of skills honed over many years of monastic maintenance work, which I always enjoyed and which I still use in other ongoing social projects.[7] It was as if events and circumstances had made the change in my life inevitable.

---

7. Generally the people amongst whom I now work have no idea of my background and probably wouldn't be interested anyhow. Though unbeknown to most, my ongoing involvement in social projects continues to be inspired by the vision of St Norbert and the original communitarian dream of Prémontré,

The change in my circumstances had many of the features of Tyrrell's own *transitus*. In fact on re-reading a life of Tyrrell I was surprised, even shocked, at how similar his view of himself and his work was to mine, with a deep sense of being compelled to pursue a path of critical honesty in the light of the challenges presented by modernity. Now I saw that whereas once I had viewed Tyrrell as a distant historical figure I found myself walking in his footsteps. His thoughts echoed my thoughts: what he wrote in 1907 of his own predicament was, ninety years later, descriptive of mine in 1997: 'I could not stay in the Roman Communion if I had to accept the Vaticanism as part of it.'

But more important for me was not so much the nature of authority as what that authority was saying and the basis on which it was saying it. For example, the new *Catechism of the Catholic Church* – with a literalist understanding of the biblical narrative of Creation, of Adam and Eve and Original Sin blurred the difference between faith and fantasy, fact and fiction – a previous more nuanced approach in a Dutch catechism had been condemned. In contrast, for me, the new science of evolutionary biology provided a much more credible narrative of why we are as we are and how our primal instincts, like our genes, continue to shape and betray us. This merely confirmed to me that I no longer thought as a Catholic.

All this now masked a deeper problem: how to understand one's own identity in a rapidly changing world of global connections, new knowledge, cultural pluralism and disparate sensitivities. This is a much greater challenge that arises for many as a consequence of modernity. Under pressure from now universalistic trends, conventional religious identity has become unstable, even an anomaly – though many choose to deny this – incompatible not so much with the content as with the structure of modern consciousness.[8] The resolution of such a challenge lies beyond any sectarian or confessional

---

so it was particularly pleasing that when one group of which I am secretary, the Friends of a large local park, recently (2014) won the Queen's Award for Voluntary Service, the citation recorded, 'This is the best example of group cohesion that I have ever come across.'

8. This is a view expressed by Charles Davis in *Religion and the Making of Society* (Cambridge, 2000), ch.8: 'Our new religious identity'. He was a prominent theologian and priest who popularised the work of the council in the 1960s but

boundary, or even cultural tradition, and for me now lay beyond the church.

In many ways I remained a creature of the 1960s with its sense of iconoclasm and adventure, change and optimism, which had also typified the Vatican Council of that era. Though it may not always have seemed that way for many, the Council had never been just about changing things so as to keep abreast of the times (*aggiornamento*). Even more importantly, it was about a reappraisal of the past (*ressourcement*) and a deepening of thought in the light of modern times (*approfondimento*). This was an altogether greater challenge, an open ended quest which I now pursued more incessantly than ever. The central issue for me was understanding the place to which modern knowledge had brought us.

Much of my general reading and interest had always been of a historical and scientific nature, particularly the earth sciences such as geology and palaeontology, which I studied at college. In fact one of the first books I remember buying at school was by the French palaeontologist and priest Teilhard de Chardin, whose *The Phenomenon of Man* was a publishing sensation of the time. It offered a visionary new attempt to reconcile scientific and religious thinking, which I found inspiring. Though not without questionable aspects – such as his predestinarian view of cosmogenesis – his thought gave a whole new dynamic dimension to traditional thinking. His concept of the next great evolutionary stage as a sphere of consciousness embracing the Earth, the 'noosphere', was certainly prophetic of the world wide web. But, just like Tyrrell before him, his life was tragically overshadowed by ecclesiastical censorship, his works banned and his thoughts constrained by silence. Another victim of modernity.

The modern era has been shaped by science. Whereas once saints directed our aspirations now scientists inform our understanding. Charles Davis once wrote that with modernity, 'although not all knowledge is scientific, that which is cognitive is often defined as that which can be objectively verified as true.' In science verification is everything. But science not only discovered new facts, invented new

---

then shocked everyone when he left the church to marry, though he continued to write on religion and modernity in a professional capacity as a distinguished academic.

things and provided new ideas, above all else it created a new reality for humanity and transformed *how* we think, as the celebrated anthropologist, Claude Levi-Strauss, wrote, 'Philosophers cannot insulate themselves against science [as clearly Pius X had tried to do]. Not only has it enlarged and transformed our vision of life … it has also revolutionised the rules by which the intellect operates.'

Darwin expressed this reality succinctly in his autobiography, noting of the evolution of his own thought, that changes in knowledge 'altered the tone of one's mind'; gradually one came to view the world differently. That is exactly how it also was with the Vatican Council: what made it different from other councils was not its dogmatic *a priori* proclamations, but its more tentative *a posteriori* explorations, which had also been the innovative style John XXIII introduced into his own pronouncements. As the Jesuit theologian, John O'Malley, wrote of the Council, it 'was unique in many ways but nowhere more than in its call for an across-the-board change in church procedures or, better, in church *style'*

It was such a style which had typified the thinking of Tyrrell and there were many who, like the notoriously reactionary Archbishop Lefebvre, saw the Council as no more than an abdication to modernism in which 'dialogue' had become the work of the devil where 'the adulterous union of the church and the (French) Revolution is cemented by "dialogue".' To anti-Modernists and neo-conservatives there has always been an element of conspiracy whereby this whole transformation was a carefully contrived plot by clandestine intellectual networks to undermine religious belief, the church and even the state. It is a useful bogeyman created to justify reaction which still thrives in the columns of *Osservatore Romano* (the Vatican newspaper) and American 'Tea Party' journals, but it is totally delusional. It is not a new conspiracy of knowledge which is the problem, it is the *consequences* of new knowledge.

For traditional ways of thinking modernity is like a 'universal acid', which dissolves everything and leaves it utterly changed. The phrase was used by the American philosopher, Daniel Dennett, to describe the effects of Darwinism, itself a key element in modern thought. It is quite a frightening metaphor. Perhaps Pope Pius was right to be frightened by its implications and seek to confront it. But the method of confrontation only produces an equally frightening alternative: the world of fundamentalism. This word and manner of thinking first appeared in America – that most modern of countries – at the same time as 'modernism' and as another form of reaction to its threat, this time within the context of the evangelical Christian churches. It has now mutated into an all too apparent reactive feature of modernity amongst all religions. What was once seen as the inevitable march of secularism has now been opposed by a religious reaction which often scorns critical thinking, asserts an intransigent traditionalism and has resurgent confidence in a higher power, God. Nothing testifies more to the arbitrary nature of belief, nor is more frighteningly modern, than the fundamentalist epitomised by the jihadist suicide bomber.

Central to this situation is an understanding of God. It is a subject about which my own views have evolved considerably, for in so far as God is the symbol of ultimate concern or order, or the embodiment of all that is connected to religion, modernity presents a particular challenge. To speak of God in a world of random natural selection, that emerged billions of years ago as the product of (perhaps) a previously collapsed universe and will end (probably) in entropic darkness, is to divest the word of any objective content or real meaning in the traditional sense. Instead, religious faith and practice has come to be regarded as a dimension of human experience, with God becoming an interior reality located in consciousness as symbol of value, hope or focus of meaning. As such, belief in God (monotheism), which was once a revolutionary and pioneering idea, has now – at least since the time of Spinoza in the seventeenth century – come to be understood as a symbol of human aspiration or the oneness of Life (monism). A sign of my gradual departure from traditional theism was an increasing interest in the SOF (Sea of Faith) network, which regards God in such a symbolic way and all religion as a human creation.

Since leaving the church, the challenge to me of modernity has widened into an attempt to find some coherent understanding of the knowledge we now have of life as a whole and of a meaningful place for humanity in it. This is an ongoing journey in search of enlightenment. Writing essays was, I found, one way of coming to terms with my thoughts. As Tyrrell also once reflected: 'It is a relief to address an inane sheet of paper,' whatever the cost of stationery. Whereas once I had preached sermons to persuade others, I now wrote essays to persuade myself, some of which are published here. Insofar as I have achieved anything in life these are what I now most value. I am sure Tyrrell would be appalled by most of what I write and the views I express. In fact I am appalled myself at some of my previous convictions and attitudes.

Their manner of composition might seem curious. An event or idea would prompt a spate of reading and research, stimulating ideas which would begin to build up like a smouldering volcano. Then a clear pattern of thought would suddenly present itself like an outpouring of lava and I would rush to get it down before it was lost. Sometimes I would awake in the middle of the night and a stream of ideas would present themselves with luminous clarity. Such was the composition of this Preface. Once, I remember, having been grappling with the issue of the random (and therefore meaningless) nature of life, I awoke in the night and the first thing that came to mind was the word 'stochastic'. This is not a common word nor one I recalled coming across before, so I got up and opened my big Collins dictionary at random and there, on the first page I opened, the first word my eye alighted on was 'stochastic'; the exact concept I had been searching for, found by the very process it described.

Sometimes people ask me what I now believe; more often than not it is a question I ask of myself. In so far as we like simple descriptive statements – as on census forms or medical registers – I can think of none and just leave them blank. This may seem strange, if not pathetic, as the presumption is that everyone has to believe in something. I believe not. For modernity, religious faith and practice are simply a dimension of human experience. In the so-called process of disenchantment that has taken humanity from belief in a divinely given cosmological and social order we have reached a point where religion as a structural principle of society has come to an end. In this state of what has sometimes been called 'post-Christianity', ironically it is Christianity, which has been seen to be 'the religion of the exit from religion', that has brought us to this point.[9] But I would not even be happy to describe myself as a post-Christian, for to me the ethical ideals of the gospels, together with the prophetic tradition of

9. M. Gauchet, *The Disenchantment of the World: A Political History of Religion* (Gallimard, 1986).

Israel, have never been surpassed and continue to represent a trans-cendental existential challenge us today. As that famous apologist for Christianity, G.K Chesterton, once quipped, it is not that Christianity has been tried and found wanting; rather, it has been found too difficult and left untried.

The invitation to produce this book came from the SOF network, which itself began as a response to the challenge of modernity and of seeking a new understanding of the place of religion and belief in the modern world. Its inspiration, Don Cupitt, is himself very much in the mould of Tyrrell – incessant in his writing, tireless in his exploration of modern thought and its implications for belief, a pursuit that has also cost him ecclesiastical preferment: the Anglican church does not normally 'do' excommunication. I had previously of-ten submitted articles for publication in the network magazine, *Sofia*, so I responded to the offer with alacrity.

Like the Bible, my book is divided into two basic sections: *Looking Back* to our beginnings and the emergence of modern thinking; *Looking Forward* to consider the effect of modernity on the way we see the world. A final section, *Here and Now*, is a sort of apocrypha of more personal reflections that tries to draw the various topics and issues together as a kind of summation. Throughout I have adopted a personal, impromptu style, which has arisen from the circumstances of writing. This impulsive nature of writing is something I also share with Tyrrell, who once wrote, 'I am always hurried to get things in … restless while anything is unfinished that I have once begun.'

My hope has always been that what I have thought and written may be of some interest to others. I do not write to expound any particular thesis nor do I lay claim to any originality; my writing is more an adventure of ideas, bringing together a wide range of think-ing from many disciplines to bear on various topics. Having said that, I do not wish just to repeat what others have written but rather, respond to them; to engage in a dialogue – the sort of dialogue envisaged by John XXIII and started over fifty years ago by the Vatican Council. Though I write with no particular expertise in any-thing, nor authority on any subject, neither is it idle conjecture: the chapter references are given to substantiate views, so that specific ideas can be located in authoritative texts.

One of the things of which I am most aware in looking back over my life is that virtually everything I have been taught or believed of any importance I have now found to be wrong. This is no bad thing in that it makes one aware that one could well be wrong again. But, insofar as this is the effect of the new knowledge of modernity, it also reveals the tentative, transient nature of modernity itself: it is forever on the point of passing away, to be overtaken by something yet more modern. The image that springs to mind is of the kaleidoscope I had as a child – each shake of the hand producing a new pattern as the disparate pieces re-form into breath-taking but fleeting arrangements.

A consequence of the individualism – or anthropological trans-cendentalism – that characterises modernity is that there is always another way of looking at things: someone else's experiences are always revelatory. What I write does not belong to any particular discipline and is certainly not theological. Since leaving the church I have lost interest in its internal theological wrangling and generally regard its reactionary views as an irrelevance.[10] The best word I can think to describe the nature of my writing is epistemic – simply knowledge of reality as we now know it in its most basic and wide-ranging form.

The content of the chapters of my book range widely with little formal structure. In a way they epitomise the ideal of the great Card-inal Newman that the product of a liberal education should be a mind that roves freely and unhindered over a vast terrain. I was privileged to have part of my education – as a trainee teacher – at an institute modelled on Newman's idea of a university and consider myself extremely fortunate to have received such a formation within the church and at the feet of many outstanding teachers, most of whom were clerics, and whose ability far outreached mine. I still look back on them with awe, such as the biblical scholar who produced the

---

10. Cf. M. Faggioli, *ibid.*, particularly ch. 4: 'The Church and the World: Augustinians and Thomists', where he discusses the neo-Augustinian tendency of wanting to set the church and world in a situation of rivals – a kind of neo-Manichaean conflict of light and dark, good and evil – in which any openness to the world is dismissed as naïve optimism. For many, if not most, people doctrinal dualism – the separation of Heaven and Earth, natural and supernatural – is what constitutes a 'religious' view of life. The religious order to which I belonged was classed as Augustinian.

definitive modern edition of the Bible or the learned Jesuit who produced his own three-volume dictionary of theology, or the other who simply dismissed an essay of mine on 'Infallibility' by pointing out I had spelt it wrong.

Just as a coda to this narrative I might add, as I began, that I write also as a victim to disability. At a very early age I contracted polio that left me partly paralysed. The effect of such an experience, of long periods of confinement, hospitalisation, and retarded education was, as I now realise, to push one to the fringes of society as something of an onlooker or outsider, an observer rather than participant. It left me with a sense of tenacious individuality. It also left me with an inclination for solitude and silence in preference to any other way of living: to be alone with my thoughts was all I asked. Perhaps it was a natural progression to desire the cloistered ways of a religious life. Its patterns and habits stay with me. These are my thoughts.

I

LOOKING BACK

CHAPTER 1

Before the Beginning

A changed view of our pre-modern origins

This reflection was prompted by a curious coincidence. Whilst visiting an elderly lady, a member of my art class, on the summer solstice our conversation drifted to Stonehenge and the mystery that surrounds both it and the origins of all our beliefs, both scientific and religious. 'We just don't know, do we?' she commented. I then went on to opine that, not only do we not know, but that looking back over my life nearly everything I had been taught or believed had turned out to be wrong. As an example I quoted how the discovery of the ancient megalith 'temples' at Gobekli Tepe – of which she had never heard – had totally changed our understanding of the origins of civilisation.[1]

Putting this assertion into context, I explained that the established historical perspective – articulated over fifty years ago by the celebrated archaeologist V. Gordon Childe – was that the so-called 'Neolithic Revolution' in farming enabled people to form settled communities, which gave them time to invent new technologies and think about the mysteries of life and thus organise religion. His '*Social Evolution*' was acclaimed by Sir Mortimer Wheeler as 'one of the landmarks in the study of the evolution of society.'[2]

As well as being an archaeologist, Childe was also a socialist who took as axiomatic the material determination of belief. For him the Neolithic Revolution – a phrase he coined – was a simulacrum of the Industrial Revolution whose technological innovation had profoundly affected social organisation and human values. This materialist view of life typified Marxist ideology: that the material infrastructure determines the spiritual superstructure. The consequent assumption of 'false consciousness' was used as to justify the

---

1. C. Mann, 'The Birth of Religion: The World's First Temple' (*National Geographic,* vol. 219, no. 6, June).
2. G. Childe, *Social Evolution* (Fontana, 1963). Foreword by Sir Mortimer Wheeler.

elimination of religious belief in the old Soviet Union. For Childe this modern ideology was the lens through which he viewed the origins of society and civilisation.

Gobekli Tepe, discovered almost by accident in the 1990s in the face of pending road works, challenged this mentality and reading of history, standing Childe's thesis on its head. In this remote part of eastern Turkey the remains of massive 'temples' by Mesolithic hunter-gatherers who, supposedly, did not even have proper tools yet could quarry, carve and erect elaborate 15-ton megaliths, ran counter to all the standard narratives of the origins of civilisation. This all took place long before there were any settlements and *seven thousand years* before the pyramids were built – the traditional starting point for histories of civilisation, before which there was deemed to be only savagery.

This discovery raised many problems for the established view of the past. To start with, just to create this site must have taken hundreds, if not thousands, of people many years so one obvious question was: how did they feed themselves? As it happens, this area is exactly the spot to which genetic research has shown that all our modern strains of wheat can be traced, resulting from the cultivation of the wild einkorn grass that (by coincidence) grows here. This indicates that cereal cultivation first happened at this precise moment in history. In other words, the demands of ritual enactment promoted not only cereal production but then also the development of a settled lifestyle and the domestication of animals, which constitute what we call the Neolithic Revolution.

We can now see that the construction of Gobekli Tepe was part of a European culture, continental in scope and of considerable sophistication, which deserves the name 'civilisation'. Forget megalith builders learning their craft from the ancient Egyptians – it was more likely the other way round.

Whilst waxing to my theme, in conversation with an increasingly bemused companion, I went on to say that this was not the half of it. The carvings on the megaliths of Gobekli Tepe are reminiscent of the cave drawings of Lascaux and Chauvet, which we had previously discussed in our art class, taking us back yet another *twenty five thousand years*. These give us yet further insight into human origins. We are now talking of what made us different from preceding hominids like the Neanderthals – not technical ability nor social organisation but ritual enactment and spiritual awareness. With this parting thought I went home, picking up a newspaper on the way.

And now for the coincidence. I opened the paper and the centre page was a magnificent double page photo of the Chauvet cave; I then opened up the computer to look up something on Amazon (unrelated to what I had been talking about) and the first book that confronted me – without any prompting – was a new study on Gobekli Tepe by Andrew Collins. I was so stunned by these coincidences that I bought it.[3]

But that was only part of it. Thanks to the super-efficient Amazon service, the book arrived the next evening and I started reading it. Whilst doing so I put on the TV to watch the new series by the Oxford mathematician, Dr. Marcus du Sautoy, on the human preoccupation with measurement: *Precision: The Measure of all Things*. I had been reading Collins's discussion of the astral orientation of the Gobekli Tepe stones, which clearly indicate the preoccupation of whoever erected them with our celestial environment, and that the latest thinking of the German scholar Michael Rappenglück was that this was also the motivation for the creation of the Lascaux paintings. Curiously, though deep underground, the paintings served as a kind of astral calendar and the animals were arranged with star clusters marked by dots next to them. As I looked up from a photo of the cave paintings in the book, to my absolute astonishment, there was du Sautoy looking at the exact same paintings in the Lascaux cave and talking about these precise markings and explaining how they formed a stellar calendar. Coincidence? Again, I was stunned.

But perhaps that is the point about everything to do with Gobekli Tepe: it is stunning. In the light of du Sautoy's remarks about the distinctly human preoccupation with understanding and ordering our environment, it is this human obsession with precision that helps to explain one of the greatest mysteries of the site: that over a period of some two thousand years each 'temple' (there are five of them in close proximity) was periodically buried – itself a herculean task –

---

3. A. Collins, *Gobekli Tepe Genesis of the Gods: The Temple Watchers and the Discovery of Eden* (Bear & Co., 2014).

and another new one built. The reason? In the successive sites the alignments of the main twin stones changes by just a few degrees (an average of four degrees) to allow for the effects of 'precession' – the change of astral locations in relation to the wobble of the Earth across a twenty six thousand year cycle. Today, by using sophisticated computer star-mapping programmes, we can see that the stones were aligned precisely to the star Deneb, in the constellation Cygnus – the celestial bird often depicted as a swan – in the Milky Way as it would have been fifteen thousand years ago. At that time Deneb would have been the brightest star of the constellation and acted as the Pole Star, the star closest to the celestial pole, the so-called turning point of the heavens. Seemingly, when the stones no longer aligned *precisely* with the constellation they were just buried and a new set erected.[4]

But why this remarkable preoccupation with the heavens? Clearly it was important for these hunter-gatherers to understand the natural rhythms of the world, the movement of the animals, the cycles of fertility and rebirth – their survival depended on such things. And not only to observe and understand it but to try and influence it through ritual enactment – shamanism. Already in Lascaux we can see depictions of such activity with a shaman, 'sorcerer', at work in ritual garb. Here, through altered states of consciousness, no doubt induced by drugs to stimulate psychotropic intoxication, they could become the birds and other animals, in order to influence the outcome of the hunt (large stone vats for beer were also found in the 'temple' enclosure). It is these same animal figures that copiously decorate the stones of Gobekli Tepe.[5]

But it was not just this life on Earth that was of concern. It was bird costume, particularly the vulture, which characterised shamanistic dress. From their ritual enactments they could hope to arise into the heavens and shape the hidden causality of life. The elaborately carved 'vulture stone' of the fourth 'temple' also reveals another

---

4. By a further amazing coincidence at the time of the events discussed the Stargazing section of *The Independent* for July focused on Deneb, the 'tail' of Cygnus the swan (30 June 2014).
5. Photos in *National Geographic, ibid.* For a detailed exploration of the mentality behind this ritual art and shamanism see David Lewis-Williams, *The Mind in the Cave* (Thames & Hudson, 2002).

story. Here the skull of a dead man, whose headless corpse is depicted at the base of the pillar, is lifted up to the heavens on the wings of a vulture, or rather shaman impersonating vulture. In this period the bodies of the deceased were placed on sky-towers – shown in other contemporary panels – for excarnation by the vultures, a practice still carried on by Zoroastrians (Parsees) and some Tibetan Buddhists. But the heads were separated and venerated whilst the bones were buried. As Anatolian prehistoric rock art expert Muvaffak Uyanik explains, 'In the Mesolithic age it was realised that man had a soul, apart from his body and it was accepted that the soul inhabited the head.'[6] The ascending vulture with the skull therefore depicts the accompaniment of the dead by its 'soul carrier' or *psychopomp* – we would call it a guardian angel – to the heavens.[7]

And not just anywhere in the heavens. The destiny was a very precise point in the Milky Way where the two 'arms' or star plumes meet to form what is called the Great Rift, a dark starless band deemed to be the portal of the eternal world. This then, it is to be presumed, was the goal of the journey that the ancestors would have to undertake on death. Everything about Gobekli Tepe, particularly the elaborately carved leaping foxes (lurking in the nearby star, Alcor) indicates that it was constructed as a theatre to effect such a transition – that this was the Cape Canaveral of Mesolithic times, which 'launched' the deceased ancestors into the heavenly afterlife.

But this is only a part of a sophisticated belief system involving a 'tiered' view of the cosmos.[8] The sky-world was seen to replicate the earth-world; its mirror image and causal mover. It is no coincidence that the star clusters – what became the signs of the zodiac – were allocated animal configurations, with Orion as their great hunter in the cosmic drama of the heavens, which recapitulated that of life on Earth. Sandwiched between the two realms, or separating them, was the thin membrane inhabited by man – a sort of Middle Earth: 'middle' not as in the temporal sequence of Middle Ages, for this was

---

6. Quoted Collins, *ibid.*
7. Further background in D. Lewis-Williams & D. Pearce. *Inside the Neolithic Mind.* (Thames & Hudson, 2005).
8. Lewis-Williams *ibid.* pp. 92 & 244 (diagrams).

a cyclical view of things, but 'middle' as in Midgard of the Norse Eddas, the earthly stage of a cosmic drama.

Vital to this drama would be the role of women and, appropriately, Gobekli Tepe means 'the hill of the navel'. Of the many so called Venus figures that come from this area and time, some show the woman giving birth to a bull. By another remarkable coincidence – and something clearly noticed by our ancient ancestors – the skull of a horned bull perfectly describes the shape of the uterus with fallopian tubes. In one of the most remarkable panels of the Chauvet Cave – graphically entitled *The Venus and the Sorcerer* – a woman's lower abdomen, with a clearly enlarged uterus, is intertwined with and overlain by a body with a bison head resting on the woman's womb. The erotic implications could not be more graphic or explicitly expressed.

The imagery of the matriarch surrounded by animals and the horned bull is found across Anatolia and Central Europe from early Neolithic times, supplementing the innumerable and much older 'Venus' figurines of the voluptuous woman that date back to the Ice Age. The site of Catal Huyuk, excavated in the 1950s by James Mellaart and dating to the eighth millennium BCE, revealed a Neolithic town, the houses of which had as a distinctive feature the adornment of the walls with bulls' heads, and beneath which the bones of the ancestors were buried in the floor – but after the heads had been removed. Mellaart speculated that the cult of the Great Goddess, who was the 'Mistress of the Animals' and later, as farming developed, presided over the agricultural cycle, was conducted by priestesses and that male priests played a minor role.[9]

The archaeologist, Marija Gimbutas, famously characterised this period as a 'gynocentric culture' in which, long before the advent of the patriarchal Aryans from the Steppes of Asia, women had an equal role with men giving rise, perhaps, to a matriarchal society, distinctive of the Neolithic age.[10] It was focused on the fearsome female huntress, before whom men trembled, and gave rise to the cult of the divine female – Diana/Artemis/Kybele – whose shrine at

9. J. Mellaart. *Catal Huyuk: A Neolithic Town in Anatolia* (Thames & Hudson, 1967).
10. M. Gimbutas, *The Goddesses and Gods of Old Europe 6,500-3,500* (Thames & Hudson, 1982).

Ephesus would become the greatest in the classical world and whose rituals still live on in the Roman Catholic cult of Mary, the divine mother, *theotokos*.[11]

In classical antiquity a new patriarchal order of civilisation, characterised by militaristic violence, sexual inequality and dualistic thinking, overturned and supressed the older order. Ironically, many of its ancient sites are now under a final threat of destruction from misogynistic Islamists. It is these same Islamists who have also tried to exterminate the Yezidis – an ancient people from this area of Gobekli Tepe, whose veneration of the Peacock Angel and belief in tribal reincarnation, lack of clergy or places of worship but periodic assembly in remote ceremonial centres, are all vestigial echoes from the distant world of Gobekli Tepe. This despised and persecuted people provide a unique link with the primal beliefs of our earliest ancestors.[12]

The two realms – of the earth world with its life-giving fertility (depicted in caves like Chauvet), and the sky world of the ancestors (to which the pillars of Gobekli Tepe point) – were seen to perfectly complement each other. When the 'Venus and Sorcerer' painting of Chauvet is overlain with a star map of the Milky Way, the woman's legs correspond *precisely* to the twin streams of the Great Rift, while the head of the bull calf in her womb corresponds to the position of the constellation Cygnus.[13] The point of entry to both womb and constellation is the star Deneb, *precisely*. Two of the 'temples' even had a sighting stone with a hole ('soul hole') also thus aligned: the stones were seemingly carved as a symbolic vulva indicating the pivotal role of the temple as a place of enacting birth, death and rebirth.

---

11. The distinctive statue of Diana, with its seemingly multiple 'breasts', has long been a source of speculation as to what exactly they represent: they could well be bulls' testicles that were draped around her effigy in offering. The ancient hymns in praise of Diana were incorporated almost unchanged into the liturgy of the Assumption of the Blessed Virgin Mary, which continues her cult as fertile Mother in subsumed form. Cf. S. Shoemaker, *Traditions of the Virgin Mary's Dormition and Assumption* (OUP 2006).
12. B. Acikyildiz, *The Yezidis: The History of a Community, Culture and Religion* (Tauris, 2014).
13. Collins *ibid.* p.74.

This perspective is reflected in numerous Neolithic burial mounds across Europe. Their layout affirms a symbolic order that represents the lower part of the female body, through which one approaches up a restricted passageway, perhaps clambering over a dynamically carved 'kerb' or 'birth' stone (as at New Grange, Northern Ireland), then by crouching or crawling, foetal-like, through the vulva-shaped opening of the barrow (dramatically so at Avening, Gloucestershire), to enter the womb-shaped belly of the mound, where the previously excarnated bones of the dead are placed – minus the head. Here, as at New Grange, the winter solstice sunlight would strike them after penetrating the shaft of the barrow.[14] The explicit sexual imagery of all this does not need further elaboration.

Today we may find the overt sexual imagery of the primal religion slightly embarrassing, if not startling. The clear implication is that just as life springs from the womb in this world, the spirits of the ancestors will be reborn from the womb of eternal life. In one startling depiction (found at Catal Huyuk, Turkey, in the period subsequent to Gobekli Tepe), the vultures which on one panel are seen to accompany the dead to heaven, bearing a skull, are shown in the next panel to be bearing a foetus back to where the skeletal remains of the dead lie; the spirit of the new-born descends from the heavens accompanied by its psychopomp/vulture/angel. The cycle of life, death and rebirth is ongoing and thus ritually re-enacted within the context of a 'tiered' cosmos.[15]

The composition of this powerful cosmology stretches back over thirty thousand years and elements would in time spread across the world to other parts of the Middle East, particularly Egypt, and as far as Meso-America. Fragments of it can be found incorporated in all the great subsequent belief systems of the world. In Egypt for example, Nut, the sky goddess who personified the Milky Way was the mother of Osiris, the god of death and resurrection, and also gave birth each morning to Re, the sun god whose effigy was a bull calf:

---

14. G. Bibby, *The Testimony of the Spade* (Fontana 1962) Also Lewis-Williams (2005) *ibid.*
15. For further background on Catal Huyuk cf. R. Rudgley, *The Secrets of the Stone Age* (Century, 2000).

seven thousand years after Gobekli Tepe the pharaohs, who claimed to incarnate the sun, would build themselves pyramids to serve the same function of ensuring their safe return to the heavens.

Echoes of this ancient cosmology are with us still in all sorts of unnoticed or forgotten ways, such as the quaint old wives tales of babies being delivered by storks or swans – northern substitutes for those vultures. As also are the sky-bird/psychopomps that in the form of eagles are emblazoned on the coats of arms of most of the old dynasties of eastern and central Europe.

What Gobekli Tepe opens up is not just a window on the heavens but a window into the human soul: what it is to be human. What set *homo sapiens* apart from their predecessors was the cognitive capacity which allowed for spiritual conceptualisation, which in turn led to collective ritualised behaviour: in other words, seeing their material environment through the prism of a cosmic worldview which they then proceeded to chart and manipulate. The purpose of ritual was spiritual empowerment and it focused on creatures that were deemed to be spiritually powerful. In time this mindset really did enable humans to master their environment, as paleo-anthropologist David Lewis-Williams writes, 'People did not invent domestication of animals for economic purposes: they did so for socio-religious ones.'[16] Similarly, with regard to the earliest form of writing – found in Turdas, western Romania from over a thousand years before its appearance in Mesopotamia – the archaeologist Richard Rudgley writes that, 'The Vinca signs seem to derive from religious rather than material concerns' and 'may be some kind of magical formulae', which were the medium for priestly activities.[17] That the earliest alphabet should arise from religious symbolism related to animal forms stands in stark contrast to the generally accepted view of its origin in practical needs.

In our scientific and technological age we tend to look at the determinants and purposes of human endeavour in materialistic terms; we view history through a prism of reductionist causality and practicality. The legacy of the Marxist archaeologist Gordon Childe is that we see a Neolithic Revolution in much the same manner as

---

16. Quoted in 'Civilisation's True Dawn' (*New Scientist,* 5 Oct 2013).
17. R. Rudgley, *Lost Civilisations of the Stone Age* (Arrow 1998).

the Industrial Revolution, which it was termed to replicate – an economically driven social transformation. Gobekli Tepe challenges that perspective. Here the motivations that drew people together were ritual, religious belief and celebration. In turn these promoted a whole raft of human endeavours: astronomy, art, and politics, then communal buildings and settled villages with their supporting technologies of pottery making, animal domestication and cereal cultivation. These were to be the seeds of civilisation; one of the most important shifts in history. But it all happened in a radically different way than was once thought, with the seeds sown by essentially spiritual and cerebral preoccupations.

Progress is a foundational 'myth' of modernity. Central to its understanding of the past is what has been called 'the march of progress' or the rise of civilisation. Our understanding of religion is often assumed to be part of this narrative with its own path of progress or ascent from animism to polytheism to monotheism, an unfolding of 'Salvation History' as in the Bible: in fact the myth of progress can itself be seen as a secularised form of Salvation History. But this is not the only way of looking at things, nor necessarily the correct one. In an important book, *The Disenchantment of the World,* the French scholar Marcel Gauchet challenged this view, stating in contrast that religion was at its most pervasive and complete form in the earliest societies, where it provided a 'structural principle' for the whole of life and society. At this point of our history the social order was not seen as established by humans but part of a preordained cosmic order. Ever since there has been an increasing attempt by humans to take control of their own destiny, to steal 'fire' from the gods – the myth of Prometheus. This process is what we now call secularisation, which results in God being drawn not only into the human world (incarnation) but then, in becoming less remote – less exterior – ultimately becoming an interior reality, located in consciousness. It is against this ineluctable process that 'organised' religion still protests, and against which priests and mullahs still rage, seeking to retain its priority as a structural principle.[18]

---

18. For an excellent discussion of this important work cf. C. Davis, *Religion and the Making of Society* (Cambridge, 1994), ch. 2: 'The Present Social Function of

Gobekli Tepe gives us a tantalising glimpse of a forgotten world. It is a pre-moral world beyond, or before good and evil: unlike in later religions morality has no place within it. Though we know so little about it, that 'little' is enough to show us that it holds a pivotal place in the drama of human history. It was here that for countless millennia humans enacted rituals, rooted in their very origins as a species, that affirmed their place in the cosmic order. It was from here, a hill overlooking Harran, that six thousand years later Abraham is reputed to have set off on his fateful wanderings.[19] It is here in this area that the biblical Garden of Eden is reputed to have been located on the fertile land between the four rivers with its abundance of animals (the home of the Mesolithic hunters who built Gobekli Tepe). It was here, after Eden and the collapse of the eco-system that sustained the Mesolithic hunters through over-hunting, man first learnt to till the soil by the sweat of his brow and where the first agriculture was practised. Oh, and lest I forget, it is here, on this hill, that there still grows a solitary 'wishing' tree scattered around which, on the ground, can still be found ancient stone carvings of finely sculpted serpents – the ancient symbol of life and knowledge. Thus began the human quest for knowledge and the long road to modernity.

Religion', in which Davis evaluates Gauchet's work, *Le Désenchantement du Monde: Une histoire politique de la religion* (1986).

19. The nearby city of Urfa was later confused with Ur of the Chaldees in Southern Mesopotamia.

CHAPTER 2

Creating a Creation Myth

How we fabricated a seminal myth and why it is no longer credible

Words are loaded things. Like freight trains they come laden with the weight of historical usage and cultural association. None more so than the word 'creation'. As we look around us that's what we see: 'creation', *every*thing. We use the same word for an act and a thing so, by inference and historic association, we have tended to believe that ultimately there must be a creator of everything. The opening passages from the Bible, giving a glimpse of the creator at work, are amongst the most powerful and influential pieces of literature ever composed. But how was 'this' created?

A Channel 4 series of personal 'takes' on the Bible set out in exploration; not with a biblical scholar, but – a more inspired choice – under the guidance of award-winning novelist and literary pundit, Howard Jacobson. With the saturnine bearing of an Old Testament prophet he confessed at the outset to being wrathful with those fundamentalists of both religion and science, who have forgotten how to 'read' this ancient story. The particular object of his wrath was Richard Dawkins, whose scientific reductionism 'moved him to fury', but also failed to recognise that the biblical account of creation represents one of the most breath-taking conceptual achievements in the history of human thought and even made science possible.[1]

But Jacobson sought a more personal, poetic approach to the creation story; one which, 'roots us in the wonder of our own being', steering us away from extreme literalism. And language is the key. It

---

1. Cf. S. L. Jaki, *Science and Creation* (Scottish Academic Press, 1974). The belief, found in Genesis, that the universe was consistent, comprehensible and 'good' would provide an essential foundation for the future Western scientific enterprise. S. Fuller. *Science vs Religion? Intelligent Design and the Problem of Evolution* (Polity, 2007) argues that the Judaeo-Christian tradition provides a unique moral motivation which made science possible.

is language which enables us to take possession of the world around us – to make it our world – and, by coincidence, this is what we find God doing: speaking as a person. Though solitary in this story, the 'gods' were always personal beings, known by their proper names before the word 'god' was invented as a generic term; created by the human imagination to explain natural phenomena.[2] By a process, ironically, akin to natural selection, there was something of an evolution from polytheism to monotheism – one supreme being as a more satisfying understanding for existence.

In search of further clarification Jacobson set out on his travels. First up was a visit to the (then) Chief Rabbi, Jonathan Sacks, to learn how Jews came by the idea of a Creator. Over a friendly cup of tea he (we) learnt how a better brand of revelation enabled Jews to banish the old gods and come up with the 'extraordinary, radical idea' of monotheism, later to be shared with Christians and Muslims.[3] This impressive achievement – in the 'family', so to speak – seemed to put a spring into the step of even an atheist. So it was off then to the epicentre of belief, Jerusalem, where we were led to believe that belief in creation had enabled Jews to come up with an even more influential idea, the seven day week. All of which, though recounted with due deliberation, is quite fatuous.

The problem for Jacobson – as for many others – was the apparent inability to look beyond his own Jewish identity to a broader cultural context. Once one makes this move, the story changes dramatically. So it was not that the seven day week was the consequence of a belief in creation but the other way round. The seven-day period is the quartering of the lunar month, the origin of which goes back

---

2. L. Geering, 'How Humans Made God', in *Reimagining God* (Polebridge, 2014).
3. Cf. J. Sacks, *The Dignity of Difference* (Continuum, 2002). A key idea of his is the 'Abrahamic umbrella', under which the three monotheistic faiths stand together. In fact this is quite fanciful and disguises the more significant issue of how religious belief evolved, for Abraham was certainly not a monotheist – an idea which only appeared in post-exilic Judaism and was subsequently redacted back into earlier texts under the name 'God'. The first mention of creation *ex nihilo* was in the Second Book of Maccabees from the second century BCE. Cf. T. L. Thompson, *The Bible in History: How Writers Create a Past.* (Jonathan Cape, 1999).

to Babylonian times.[4] Celebrations of the full moon also provide the likely root of the word Sabbath, the seven-day creation story being a later manipulation to confer significance on the Sabbath with the first chapter of Genesis among the very last to find its way into the Bible (probably about the 4th century BCE). The astral basis for celebrations commencing on the eve, marked by the rising of the stars, probably goes back at least to Neolithic times.[5]

As for the more substantial issue of the creation story itself, one has to look to the alien cultural context Jews were forced to endure in the sixth century during the Babylonian Exile. Jacobson considered this traumatic period as a time when Jewish beliefs in God had seemingly been discredited and needed some new markers of religious identity to rejuvenate the demoralised community, but he entirely missed its real significance. Not only did Jews pick up the format of many key 'biblical stories' which appear in Genesis from their sojourn in the East, but when they returned to Palestine their Judaism was significantly different from what went before.[6]

There were now radically different organisational structures – centred on synagogues and rabbis – and also beliefs. Judaism also took on a distinctly eschatological tone, characterised by beliefs in the cosmic moral conflict of good and evil, the idea of a final judgment, the mediation of angels and a final apocalyptic coming of a righteous one (messiah). All of these beliefs were foreign to and predated Judaism, though they later came to characterise it. They arose in Persia under the influence of Zoroastrianism, where they were accompanied by belief in one supreme solar being, who resided in the heavens but was also the creator of all. Far from being a dualistic faith, the universal nature of Ahura Mazda, the supreme deity,

---

4. *Encyclopedia Judaica:* 'Sabbath', also J. P. McEvoy, *A Brief History of the Universe* (Running Press, 2010) and also S. Toulmin & J. Goodfield, *The Fabric of the Heavens.* (Harper & Row, 1964).

5. Cf. *National Geographic* (Jan. 2004) article on the recently discovered Neolithic 'sky disc' for locating astral points: ancient ceremonial sites had sophisticated orientations to the rising of stars cf. D. Lewis-Williams & D. Pearce, *Inside the Neolithic Mind* (Thames and Hudson, 2005).

6. S. Sand, *The Invention of the Jewish People* (Verso, 2009) ch. 3: 'The Invention of the Exile'.

entitles Zoroaster's teachings to be viewed as the first real intimations of monotheism.[7]

When the Jews returned home from the East after 538 BCE, they found themselves further exposed to another powerful current of new thinking, this time from the West – from the Aegean, where Greek thinkers such as Thales and Anaximander had, from the beginning of the sixth century, been speculating on the rational principles underlying the cosmos. This esoteric form of natural philosophy, based on rational explanation, became the precursor of what we now know as 'science'. It was like an acid to the older Homeric world of chaotic polytheism and in place of a capricious cosmos ruled by unpredictable immortals, it provided the seminal idea of an ordered, comprehensible, coherent *uni*-verse. This sublime monism found expression in Platonism and rapidly spread with trade and Hellenism across the Middle East.[8]

It is from these disparate elements that the new God of Jewish monotheism became possible and it also made possible a theology of creation, a theology that was more philosophical than religious. None of this was mentioned by Jacobson, whose biblical fare was proffered unadulterated. What was also not acknowledged was that the seemingly fluent narrative of God in the Bible was a late and highly contrived literary device. As the literary guru, Harold Bloom, pointed out in his biblical mimesis *The Book of J*, 'Archaic Judaism is all but totally unknown to us...All I can see is that (it) has very little to do with the God of Ezra or the God of Akiba.'[9] What we see is now visible only through the lens of the greatest fictional character in literature: God. It was the retrospective power of this later, new idea that was formative of the Bible as we now know it. Perhaps the best metaphor for this process is a geological one: the books and traditions of the Bible accumulated like great sedimentary layers over the centuries, finally to be metamorphosed and welded into one by the power of its last and greatest idea, monotheism.

---

7. P. Kriwaczek, I*n Search of Zarathustra: The First Prophet and the Ideas that Changed the World* (Weidenfeld & Nicolson, 2002).
8. A. N. Whitehead, *Adventures of Ideas* (Simon & Schuster, 1933).
9. H. Bloom, *The Book of J* (Faber & Faber, 1991).

It is not without note, and surely no coincidence, that writing and the possibility of narrative arose in the same cultural milieu as monism and monotheism. As Walter Ong wrote, 'writing restructures consciousness.'[10] At first only a means of recording and ordering produce, writing began to release its hidden potential for the recording and ordering of ideas.[11] It is interesting that in the creation story a key word is *hivdil*, divide. God is presented as dividing the light and dark, sea and land, etc. – everything is being sorted out, just as a scribe would, introducing order where before there had been chaos. And just as the accountant scribe sorted out his records, so there was the potential for critical reflection on stored information and ideas, thus providing a stimulus to abstract thought.

In his study of *The Origins of the Modern Mind*, Merlin Donald saw this as a final decisive stage in the evolution of human consciousness[12] – though modern information technology may now be providing another stimulus to further neurological development. The creation story not only reassured a traumatised refugee community, it fulfilled a fundamental human need, to have things ordered and comprehensible. In other words, the story reflects not so much reality but the human needs which at a certain point in human development created this supreme symbol of order: God.

Though we tend to take this ubiquitous word for granted now as understood, in fact it has no clear meaning.[13] It is a concept we struggle with. Just like Jacob at the ford of Jabbok we seem to be locked in constant struggle with an unseen assailant. Don Cupitt sagely noted that the idea of an individual God is inextricably linked with the rise of 'a more individuated human selfhood'.[14] In acting as the mirror by which we come to look at ourselves, God and human subjectivity are born together. In the same way creation is not

---

10. W. Ong, *Orality and Literacy* (Routledge, 1992) quoted by J. Sacks, in an interesting discussion of the implications of literacy, *ibid.* pp 130-131.
11. R. Rudgley, *Lost Civilisations of the Stone Age* (Arrow, 1998) for a detailed discussion of the origins of writing (chs.3-5) and the seminal work of Denise Schmandt-Besserat.
12. M. Donald, *The Origins of the Modern Mind: Three Stages in the Evolution of Culture and Cognition* (Harvard, 1991)
13. M. Henry, *On Not Understanding God* (Maynooth Press, 1997) for an exhaustive study.
14. D. Cupitt, *After God: The Future of Religion* (Weidenfeld & Nicolson, 1997).

something that happened but is happening, now. It is a drama in which we are involved and which is about us, happening now, as life for ever threatens to teeter back into chaos. Interestingly, this was the understanding of Jacobson's sister as she explained the lighting of the Sabbath candles.

These are subtle and profound concepts and it is often forgotten that while the first pages of the Bible – and the ideas they contain – were amongst the last to be written, they cast a surreal afterglow over many of its later (earlier) pages. In fact, it seems highly ironic in terms of the present conflict between creationist and evolutionist that the Bible, far from being monolithic, is itself a product of evolution and as with any composite structure, when one looks closely all sorts of incongruities emerge, which betray a divergent past.

So, after a sonorous opening the theme of monotheism gets entangled in more ancient beliefs: Abraham's family are found fussing over their fertility figurines (an archaeologist provided some for Jacobson to finger), there is the shady El Shaddai, the former fertility god 'of the breasts', and evil Moloch to whom, long after Solomon's temple had supposedly been built, the inhabitants of Jerusalem were still sacrificing their first-born outside the city walls. It is amongst this motley of tribal beliefs of the ancient Israelites that Dawkins finds his nasty, brutish and genocidal god. These earlier beliefs remain embedded in the narrative that later redactors did not bother to remove, leaving us now with some difficult explanations.

A recent example of this problem arose with the publication in 1966 of the Jerusalem Bible. Under the sagacious influence of biblical scholars it was decided to replace 'God' by 'Yahweh' in many parts of the text, much to the mystification of the public, which had never come across the word before. For enlightenment they were informed that this was the supreme revelation of the divine being to Moses in the sublime event at the burning bush. More recently, in a remote part of the Sinai desert at an ancient travellers' way station, archaeologists found bits of broken pottery inscribed with names like 'Yahweh of Teman and his Asherah' and even with crude graffiti befitting any public toilet with a gawky fellow sporting a large penis next to his consort – obviously some tribal fertility god.[15] No wonder Bloom irreverently notes that, 'Yahweh constitutes one of the curious cultural comedies of Western religious tradition.'[16]

Regardless of this, back in his home town of Manchester, Howard Jacobson had decided to visit the in-laws, – two of whom were Orthodox rabbis – for further enlightenment on the clash between the findings of science and religious beliefs. Not that it seemed a problem: one rabbi acknowledged he would always believe the teaching of his religion 'implicitly' and the other dismissed rational speculation as feeble next to strong belief. To this conversation stopper to the inquiring mind there is no answer, other than the sort of derisive dismissal of the self-contradictions implicit in 'strong belief' that Spinoza provided: if belief entails us accepting a supreme being who is almighty and benign, how do we explain evil which he is either not good enough or strong enough to stop? Various attempts to resolve this paradox, such as by a chief rabbi in Jerusalem, Ovadia Yosef – who explains the Holocaust as a punishment for sin – is no more than a cue for outrage and incredulity.

Clearly, there are problems that the serene simplicity of the creation story does not address in terms of its later relation to science and modern knowledge. But then it was never intended to, so that fundamentalists are now radically misinterpreting it. The genre of ancient myths, to which the creation story belongs, were the expression of humans struggling to find meaning and their place in the world; the existential questions which hang in the unknown: who are we? What shall we become? Where are we going? To these questions there are no final answers. In her *Short History of Myth* Karen Armstrong writes that, 'A myth is true because it is effective, not because it gives us factual information.'[17] Myth is an art form not science; it tells us about *ourselves,* not some trans-historical reality.

---

15. Discussed, with pictures, in H. Shanks, *The Mystery and Meaning of the Dead Sea Scrolls* (Random House, 1998).
16. H. Bloom, *ibid.* p. 23. Bloom also, provocatively, always refers to the author of the text as 'she'.
17. K. Armstrong, *A Short History of Myth* (Canongate, 2005) p.10.

It was to this sort of understanding that Jacobson felt himself drawn: it is also the point at which we can escape the impasse between religious and scientific fundamentalisms. For Jacobson it was the poetic world of creativity, surrounded by 'doubt, uncertainty, mystery' that was the most important aspect of myth. Paradoxically, this is also the point to which modern scientific knowledge has also brought us to once more. Between the infinitely small and infinitely large, between the quantum world and cosmic black holes, there are incomprehensible worlds, which we will never be able to comprehend. With our limited senses we are attuned to just one narrow band of reality, but there is reason to believe there is more, much more, of which we will never know. Science has relativised and diminished us in the world of post-modernity.

The modern problem is that the ancient myths no longer *work* for us. In order to work, myth must lead us into deeper understanding of reality, perhaps forcing us to change our minds and the way we live. But the ancient creation myth no longer seems to do this: it simply conflicts with reality, as we now understand it, rather than leading us into it; instead of leading to enlightenment it has the opposite effect – it obscures reality by negating the knowledge we have. In the modern narrative of cosmology 'creation' has now simply become 'everything', its mythological origin a 'theory of everything': we are not even sure that we live in one *uni*-verse.[18]

The world of the ancient myths is not our world. Of key elements of the creation story we now know that there is no necessary point of beginning; that species are not fixed in isolation but all part of the seamless web of life; that humans are not set apart but inextricably linked by their DNA to all other creatures; that life is not 'morally' good but an amoral struggle which is often savage and remorseless; that the creation of life is ongoing regardless of us and will continue after us; that extinction is a vital part of the process.

But we still need myths and are still fertile myth-makers; there is the myth of progress, the myth of racial superiority, the Freudian myth of the tripartite self (the id, ego and super-ego), Gaia theory is a modern creation myth. Such thinking enables humans to find meaning and to order their worlds. One of the more curious, and

18. J. Barrow, *The Book of Universes* (Bodley Head, 2011).

perhaps unexpected, features of our times is the way in which belief has defiantly set aside the implications of science when it invades our comfort zone: knowledge of climate change, for example, is given little credence when it challenges our fossil fuel economies. The assumption that somehow science would bring with it the thinking and values of modernity has not happened as expected.

The men who flew planes into the twin towers all had a scientific background but they certainly didn't have the values of modernity. Similarly, the pseudo-science of Intelligent Design manipulates modern research to underpin creationist ideology. The paradoxical thing in all this is that, as the biblical scholar Thomas Thompson writes, 'The Bible's theology is not a theology of truths. It is a way of critical reflection. It is learning and discourse.'[19] It was through critical reflection on later experience that biblical material was recast and re-edited. In turn the process of critical reflection has become the most distinctive feature of Western civilisation and most profound consequence of biblical thinking.[20] It is not a finished process, yet it is this central feature of the bible that is discarded in modern controversies by the very people who claim to follow its guidance. Biblical belief has become a deracinated ideology, even a form of idolatry, which Lloyd Geering calls 'bibliolatry', with its adherents desperately clinging on to it as a life raft.

The same can now be said of monotheism itself. Once a unifying symbol affirming the unity of the *uni*-verse, it is now continuing to evolve as a concept beyond the image of a personal being, God, leaving the *theism* and becoming a simple *monism*. This is the 'coming of age', of which Bonhoeffer prophetically spoke, of godless religion. And with it comes fear, fear of our own responsibility. But fear of change only fossilises the past; as Nietzsche, always keenly attuned to the contradictions of our modern condition, had perceptively noted in *The Birth of Tragedy*, 'The mythic premises of a religion are systematised, beneath the stern and intelligent eyes of an orthodox

19. Thomas L.Thompson, *The Bible in History: How Writers Create a Past* (Jonathan Cape, 1999,)p. 249.
20. D. Cupitt. *The Meaning of the West* (SCM, 2008) for a penetrating study of this theme.

dogmatism, into a fixed sum of historical events; one begins nerv-
ously defending the veracity of myths, at the same time resisting their
continuing life and growth.' Thus religions become sclerotic and
lifeless.

What is now required is a continuation of that process of critical
reflection which typified the biblical tradition itself in its formative
period. The sort of thing rabbi Lionel Blue did so well in his daily
radio presentations. It was whilst reflecting on growing up in the East
End of London during the war that he tells the story of his religiously
observant parents who always separated everything according to
orthodox tradition – *hivdil* again, dividing as on the day of creation.
That was until the German bombs came and blew everything to
pieces; since then in his own personal life, as in modern society, it
has been a matter of sorting out the bits and making a meaning out
of the mess, order out of chaos. As it was in the beginning, the
process is ongoing.

CHAPTER 3

Regarding Nature Anew

From natural theology to a 'theology' of nature

For the past four centuries natural theology has been a very English preoccupation. In its search for a way between the Scylla of Roman Catholic theological authoritarianism and the Charybdis of Puritan biblical literalism the framers of the Elizabethan Settlement in the sixteenth century saw natural theology as the ideal basis for a *via media*. In his influential *Laws of Ecclesiastical Polity,* the Anglican divine, Richard Hooker, argued that by turning to reason and evidence all men of good will could find sufficient truth about the Creator; all that was needed was a little observation of nature, for, 'Nature and Scripture do serve in such full sort that they both jointly and not severally either of them be so complete that unto everlasting felicity we need not the knowledge of anything more than these two may easily furnish.'[1]

Such a view harmonised admirably with that of Hooker's contemporary, Sir Francis Bacon, who was setting out his own empirical agenda for the advancement of knowledge, on a similar basis of the accurate observation of nature.[2] Thus appeared a new breed of

---

1. Quoted M. Ruse, *Darwin and Design* (Harvard, 2003) p. 36.
2. The growth of Puritanism in the seventeenth century also encouraged the scrupulous recording not only of events but attempts in the discernment of spirits to identify causes and consequences, all recorded in 'methodical' (a Puritan catchword) diaries of great detail, which was quite a new phenomenon; natural theology and natural philosophy (also based on meticulous recordings), spiritual 'method' and experimental method thus became two sides of the same coin, witness the predominance of clerics in the founding of the Royal Society (the world's first 'scientific' institute) and the fashion for such subjects as 'Political Arithmetic' devoted to the inquiry into economic progress – spiritual and material advancement were also seen to be complementary as well as being signs of providential 'Justification'. Cf. R.H. Tawney, *Religion and the Rise of Capitalism* (Pelican, 1922), ch.4: 'The Puritan Movement', also the BBC4 series by Adam Nicolson on the English Enlightenment (2014).

clergyman-naturalist, such as John Ray (1628-1705).[3] The title of his major work, *Wisdom of God, Manifested in the Words of Creation* (1691) really says it all. The living world is the work of the supreme designer, 'There is no greater, at least not more palpable and convincing argument of the Existence of a Deity, than the admirable Art and Wisdom that discovers itself in the Make and Constitution…of Heaven and Earth.'

Henceforth, and by happy coincidence, the advancement of knowledge could be co-opted for the glorification of God. Such would be the purpose of natural theology. That there might have been a serpent lurking in the undergrowth of such ambition does not seem to have occurred to anyone; but it should surely have suggested itself from the pages of scripture itself on the temptation to search for knowledge. That there might be a disjunction between knowledge and faith, observation and revelation first became apparent to Thomas Burnet, a Cambridge scholar and royal chaplain to Charles II. Whilst taking a trip through the Alps, its rugged terrain of 'indigested heaps of Stones and Earth' prompted him to reflect on how such 'confusion came into Nature.' Surely the Creator wouldn't have left things in such an unreasonable mess so perhaps there was some further explanation.

In his *Sacred Theory of the Earth* Burnet argued that it was all a result of the Flood, which had necessitated the defacement of the original creation. If he thought that this would now cleverly harmonise observation and revelation, the storm of outrage that his theory caused prompted him to think otherwise. For the newly sanguine natural theology held that the world was not 'a great Ruine', defiled by human sin, but a wondrous creation expressly designed by God for the edification and convenience of His favourite species. There had been no 'second thoughts'. But the nub of the issue for Burnet's critics was that his loose reading of scripture, so as to coincide with observation, would only encourage scepticism in the irreligious: as

---

3. K. Thomson, *The Watch on the Heath: Science and Religion before Darwin* (Harper Collins, 2005).

one churchman put it, 'That way of philosophising all from Natural Causes I fear will turn the whole World into Scoffers.'[4]

This prescient remark was a portent of things to come. The more carefully naturalists observed the Earth, the odder it all seemed to be. It was with the emergence of the new science of geology in the eighteenth century that the cracks in the edifice of natural theology first began to appear. By the end of that century they had become gaping chasms. It was particularly through the study of what we now call fossils – for long it was unclear what exactly these 'things' dug from the ground (Latin: *fossilis*) actually were – that it became apparent that the world was not only far older than ever envisaged by scripture but that whole worlds had come and gone, inhabited by demonic creatures (dinosaurs). These, according to one clergyman were, 'armed with the virility of Evil … a teeming Spawn fitted for the lowest abysm of Chaos.'[5]

To the faithful and generality of the populace such discoveries brought great disquiet and raised disturbing questions: if (and for a long time it was contested that it was only an 'if') such creatures had indeed existed they could only be the work of the devil. A good God could have no time for such disgusting and pointless creatures. It was only after much hesitation, and before languishing into insanity, that the first holder of Oxford's chair of geology (created with the explicit purpose of strengthening the scientific basis of belief), the Reverend William Buckland, was forced to admit that such a world had indeed existed and was 'inconsistent with a Creation founded in Benevolence.'[6]

Buckland was a colourful character, given to concluding popular lectures on fossils with the singing of the national anthem in thanks for vital minerals, such as coal, which, 'express the most clear design of Providence to make the inhabitants of the British Isles, by means of this gift, the most powerful and richest nation on Earth.' This

---

4. Discussed in R. Macfarlane, *Mountains of the Mind* (Granta, 2003); see also D. Montgomery, *The Rocks Don't Lie* (Norton, 2012) for a more detailed discussion, particularly ch.4: 'World in Ruins'.
5. D. Cadbury, *The Fossil Hunters* (Fourth Estate, 2000).
6. Cadbury, *ibid.* Modern day creationists have now redeemed the situation by having dinosaurs in the Garden of Eden, thus correcting a biblical oversight. Cf. Montgomery, *ibid.* ch.10: 'Dinosaurs in Paradise'.

belief in a Special Providence, beneficial to the nation, was already widespread in the eighteenth century, popularised to a credulous public by antiquarians such as William Stukeley.[7] It was a view which would also take deep root in England's American colonies – where it still thrives. Obviously everything had been designed with our, sometimes very specific, interests in mind.

If, in the larger picture of natural theology there was no justification for such beliefs, then where indeed would it lead not only scoffers but the devout? As a case in point, when the one time aspirant to Holy Orders, Charles Darwin, visited Galapagos, what he observed undermined his belief in the very premise of natural theology: for the 'God of Galapagos' showed himself to be careless, wasteful, indifferent and almost diabolical – certainly not the sort of God to whom anyone would be inclined to pray.[8] Indeed, the more deeply Darwin pondered and investigated, the more remote seemed the possibility of any providential guidance of nature at all.

The high water mark of natural theology was undoubtedly reached in the work of William Paley, *A View of the Evidences of Christianity* (1794). It was of Paley's works that Darwin wrote with such affection in his autobiography of his time at Cambridge: 'The careful study of these works ... was the only part of the Academic Course which, as I then felt and still believe, was of the least use to me in the education of my mind.'[9] It was therefore highly ironic that the first casualty of the new theory of 'natural selection' should be the natural theology of Paley's argument from design. But Darwin was emphatic, 'There seems to me no more design in the variability of organic beings ... than the course which the wind blows.'[10] Yet, as the famous final paragraph of *The Origin of Species* indicates, as Darwin stands contemplating 'an entangled bank', there is more than just a struggle for life going on, there is also 'a grandeur' in the view of nature as a whole.[11]

---

7. S. Piggott, *Ancient Britons and the Antiquarian Imagination* (Thames & Hudson, 1989).
8. E. Larson, *Evolution's Workshop: God and Science on the Galapagos Islands* (Penguin, 2001).
9. C. Darwin, *Autobiographies* (Penguin Classics, 2002), p.31.
10. Darwin, *ibid.* p. 50.
11. C. Darwin, *The Origin of Species* (Wordsworth Classics, 1998), p.368.

It is at this point, according to the philosopher Michael Ruse, that in the 1870s, 'natural theology took a wrong if understandable turn' in not only abandoning the argument from design but the argument from complexity on which it is based. It is the ever-increasing organic complexity pervasive in the natural world, and man's place within it, that might still suggest some overall 'final cause' or at least something beyond the provenance of science. All of which means, for Ruse, 'that we have to rethink the relation of humans to the rest of the world... But not in a condescending theological fashion.'[12]

This view is supported by Fritjof Capra in his study of the development of European scientific thought, *The Turning Point*. Because of the focus on individual organisms and species, he writes, 'The creative unfolding of life towards forms of ever increasing complexity remained an unsolved mystery for more than a century after Darwin.'[13] It is something that a more holistic view of systems theory, that focuses on the dynamics of self-organisation and the role of the environment, has now remedied with such concepts as 'ecosystem' or 'bio-diversity'.[14]

Meanwhile, in society at large, the agenda of Bacon and the enthusiasm of the new natural scientists had led to the emergence of a wholly new kind of industrialised society in which the new knowledge and exploitation of nature's resources – regarded as a source of endless beneficence – was becoming insatiable, destructive and unsustainable. It was John Ruskin who complained about the consequent destruction the human spirit and of belief: 'those dreadful Hammers!' he complained of the new science of geology which threatened biblical certainties, 'I hear the clink of them at the end of every cadence of the Bible verses.' He too lapsed into depressive dementia.

Clearly something was very wrong. It was not long before questions began to be raised about the very foundational principles

12. Ruse, *ibid.* p.112.
13. F. Capra, *The Turning Point: Science, Society and the Rising Culture* (Flamingo, 1982), p. 313.
14. E. Wilson, *The Diversity of Life* (Penguin, 1992); also S. Kauffman, *At Home in the Universe: The Search for the Laws of Complexity* (Penguin, 1995).

of this modern civilisation. The distinguished historian Arnold Toynbee wrote, 'Some of the major maladies of the present world – in particular the recklessly extravagant consumption of nature's irreplaceable treasures, and the pollution of those that man has not already devoured – can be traced back to a religious cause, and this cause is the rise of monotheism.'[15] It seemed that the Western 'religion of modern times' (Christianity) had first robbed nature of its mystery, then insisted that it was God's will that man exploit nature for his own ends and then encouraged the growth of a destructive scientific mentality, which now threatened to destroy not only nature but humanity as well.

And there was something else. Just as the ecological implications of this religion had not been recognised, neither had another feature: its patriarchalism. As the feminist theologian Mary Daly wrote, 'Where God is male, the male reigns supreme.'[16] By the nineteenth century women were beginning to challenge the assumptions and values of a society run largely by men for men. Nor did it take much insight to realise that the whole edifice of natural theology was a very male affair. Like women, the Earth had always been regarded as feminine in its fecundity and, like women, the male view was that both were there for man's pleasure and exploitation. Bacon had spoken enthusiastically of wresting nature's secrets from her – in other words the rape of the Earth.

A feminine view of nature as the source of fertility was something regarded with suspicion from the outset of monotheism: the Bible simply designated the ancient goddess of fertility, Ashtoreth, as 'shame' and nature cults as an abomination. In Christian times the ancient pagan rites of nature were partly absorbed into cultic practices – such as making Mary the 'Queen of the May', which had nothing to do with the original teaching of Christianity – or condemned as 'witchcraft'. But the consequences of the apparent

---

15. Quoted in L. Geering. *The Greening of Christianity* (St. Andrew's Trust, 2005), an incisive examination of the role of Christian belief in contributing to the current ecological crisis and the changes in belief now needed.
16. M. Daly, *Beyond God the Father* (Beacon Press, 1973).

dualism implicit in Christian theology, whereby the natural was subverted to the supernatural – this 'dirty little world' to the 'heavenly Jerusalem' – was clearly becoming untenable.

The cumulative effect of such profound cultural reappraisals has been to propel theological thought about nature onto a new level of understanding. As the theologian Lloyd Geering wrote, 'Our growing knowledge of how life has evolved, and of the earthly parameters within which all creatures live, has amounted to a new revelation that supplements and largely replaces the supposed revelation of the past.'[17] The heart of this new 'revelation' is what is now called 'green consciousness'. It was epitomised by the American Catholic priest Thomas Berry when he wrote in *The Dream of the Earth*, 'There is an awe and reverence due to the stars in the heavens, the sun and heavenly bodies; to the seas and the continents; to all living forms of trees and flowers; to the myriad expressions of life in the sea; to the animals of the forest and birds of the air.'[18] This is an awe and reverence that is due to them in their own right, not merely as a means to an end, either theological or practical. He went on to warn that, 'To wantonly destroy a living species is to silence forever a divine voice.'

Here we glimpse the emergence (evolution?) of a new kind of theology: a theology of nature. Unlike the previous natural theology it sees nature simply in terms of itself, as an inviolable, mysterious 'other' which makes its own epiphanies. In his Gifford Lectures of 1953, devoted to the theological implications of the new understanding of nature, Canon Charles Raven – amongst the last of that great tradition of clerical naturalists – captured something of this spirit when he wrote of his sheer pleasure in observing butterflies, 'Every specimen different from the rest ... To move from one to another, to sense the difference of impact, to work out the quality of this difference in the detailed modifications of the general pattern, this was a profoundly moving experience.'[19]

---

17. Geering, *ibid.*
18. T. Berry, *The Dream of the Earth* (Sierra Club Books, 1988).
19. C. Raven, *Natural Religion and Christian Theology: Experience and Interpretation* (Cambridge, 1953).

If the 1870s were a time of crisis for natural theology, the 1970s were a time of radical change in our understanding of nature. Rachel Carson had already sounded a solitary warning in her book *Silent Spring* over the use of pesticides. Dismissed as 'so much hogwash', it dared to challenge the destructive consequences of the pursuit of progress, which, in a word, was 'killing' the Earth. Then something more visually dramatic happened: we started getting pictures of the Earth from the Apollo spacecraft: a small blue globe of sublime beauty hovering in the vast abyss of the universe. This was our planet, all we had – so small, so vulnerable in the black emptiness of space, and we were destroying it.

Gradually, a new awareness arose of our planet as a self-contained life raft and it was given a name, Gaia, after the Greek goddess of the Earth. James Lovelock's Gaia theory of planetary self-regulation helped pave the way for New Age mystics and environmental activists.[20] As a species we now understood ourselves to be part of a vibrant and almost inexhaustibly wondrous complex web of life that surrounded the Earth like a delicate membrane: what another clergyman-cum-scientific mystic, Teilhard de Chardin, called the 'biosphere'. His 'law of complexity' – describing the increasing complexity of matter that had led ineluctably to the emergence of consciousness – seemed to suggest a 'directionality' in nature. But the truly awesome thing was that now, small as we are, we have the power not only to comprehend all this but to destroy it – and ourselves with it.

This awareness brought with it a sense of urgency to reconnect with the natural world. It was expressed in the title of Sally Mc-Fague's book, *Super, Natural Christians: How we should Love Nature*.[21] For her the ecosphere has now become the focus for an ecological theology; an incarnational theology with a difference: now 'The body of God is not a body but all the different, peculiar, particular bodies about us.' The divine is to be found all around us in the ecosphere. In this new dispensation there has been a metamorphosis of the old religious vocabulary, which can be confusing but which is also in-structive: 'salvation' is now about saving the planet, 'sanctuaries' are

---

20. J. Lovelock, *The Ages of Gaia* (Norton, 1988).
21. S. McFague, *Super, Natural Christians* (Fortress Press, 1997).

those last refuges of wilderness, Life has become co-terminous with God.[22]

In a sense we are now living between two stories of nature. While we are still trying to accept the implications of the new, evolutionary story, much of the old story lingers on in our thinking and language. It is a bit like the vehicles one sometimes see in Third World countries, festooned with all sorts of medallions, charms and statues: if one breaks down who do you call upon, the gods or a mechanic? Lloyd Geering comments perceptively that this transition replicates that great transition from polytheism to monotheism: it wasn't achieved overnight nor without much controversy – in fact it began in what has been called the Axial Period of the sixth century BC and is still going on. But it triumphed because it was a superior idea. Now it is being replaced by a yet more persuasive idea, monozoism – the oneness of life.[23]

The new era in which humanity now finds itself has been given a new name: the anthropocene – the era in which humanity shapes the future of the planet.[24] It opens a new chapter in the Earth's geological and biological history with humanity as the dominant force. It is also a potentially destructive force with its nuclear capability and spiralling population. Already the 'fossil-industrial' complex threatens the planet's life systems and humans, together with the domesticated animals on which their survival depends, account for 97% of the biomass of all the larger animals combined, while wild animals are a mere 3%. This overwhelming and unprecedented dominance of the planet by one species requires a wholly new attitude to nature, if we are to survive, one in which we must recognise our symbiotic relationship with nature, rather than the current parasitic one which regards nature as an 'externality' to be exploited as an inexhaustible resource or useful sump in which to deposit our waste. In the new mentality of the anthropocene age there is no longer a dualism of

---

22. D. Cupitt, *The New Religion of Life in Everyday Speech* (SCM, 1999) and *Life, Life* (Polebridge, 2003).
23. L. Geering. *Reimagining God* (Polebridge, 2014), ch. 14: 'Spirituality for an Ecological Age'.
24. C. Schwägerl, *The Anthropocene: The Human Era and how it Shapes our Planet* (Synergetic Press, 2015); also 'Time to Play God' (article, *The Independent*, 25.2.2015).

'nature' and 'culture', nature and super-nature: the environment becomes the '*in*vironment', something in which humans are existentially interwoven, not something 'out there' with which we co-exist, but something in which we inhere in co-dependency. In order to survive, human civilisation will have to function as an integral part of the biosphere in a sustainable and ecologically sensitive way.

The demands of such a new way of life and thinking are daunting. The alternative of pretending we can go on as we are in our abusive relationship with nature will be disastrous. Fundamental will be a new sense of respect and humility, the sense of awe which Rudolf Otto once famously described as being at the root of the idea of holiness, an awe which many feel in the presence of the mystery and majesty of nature. Call it Nature Mysticism, Green Christianity, neo-paganism or whatever, the new 'theology' of nature now incorporates all that we have learned about the human species and the natural world. 'Life' has become the new metaphor for 'God' as the ultimate symbol of totality. In this sense it is still possible to talk of a 'theology' of nature. Now, as the theologian Gordon Kauffman wrote, 'To believe in God is to commit oneself to a particular way of ordering one's life and action. It is to devote oneself to working towards a fully humane world within the ecological restraints here on planet Earth, whilst standing in piety and awe before the profound mysteries of existence.'[25] Such is the basis of the new 'theology' of nature.

---

25. G. Kaufman. *In the Face of Mystery* (Harvard, 1993).

CHAPTER 4

Daring to Look at Reality

How 'natural philosophers' changed our view of the world

In 1772 a little known Welsh landscape painter, Thomas Jones, had reached Naples after nearly a decade travelling around Italy. In the quiet of the afternoon siesta he opened the shutters of his lodgings and, perhaps in a moment of tedium, just painted the walls and roofs of the buildings opposite. The air of ordinariness which exudes from the rectangles and diagonals of the buildings, painted to postcard size, has all the features of a modern, everyday sort of photographic print we now take for granted; which is what makes it so revolutionary.[1]

Jones went on to paint a number of other such 'nondescript' pieces before returning to Britain, where he was duly forgotten. Two hundred years later they have made Jones's name. By Classical standards they are pictures of absolutely nothing – no people or postures, no composition or 'view', no style or story: just what happened to be there. In this they represent a pictorial revolution, tutoring the eye to see what is before it without pretext or pretence.

By curious coincidence, as Jones was painting his pictures, a little known Scottish gentleman farmer, James Hutton, was touring Britain looking at rock outcrops.[2] What particularly interested him was the way vertical beds of rock suddenly became overlaid with horizontal beds of rock, creating what looked like pieces of geometrical abstract art. Hutton's explanation was that such rock formations could only have resulted from successive cycles of erosion and deposition over

---

1. An exhibition of his work, under the title *Thomas Jones in Italy*, took place at the National Gallery in 2003.
2. Cf. S. Baxter, *Revolutions in the Earth* (Weidenfeld & Nicolson, 2003) for a biography of James Hutton.

vast periods of time. By observing what was before him and suggesting a plausible explanation he would cause outrage and change our understanding of the world.

Hutton published his views in a work entitled *Theory of the Earth* – a book which would become one of the cornerstones of the new science of geology. It was not very well written; like Jones's paintings, it would probably soon have been forgotten, had not friends re-edited the work. The ensuing storm of outrage arose from the suggestion that the rocks of the Earth were formed over an unimaginable period of time. In doing so it challenged the commonly held view of biblical chronology that the Earth was only some 6000 years old. Hutton was duly labelled an atheist – which he was not – and his views ridiculed. One such attack, entitled, *The Character of Moses Established for the Veracity as an Historian, Recording Events from the Creation to the Deluge*, gives a flavour of what he was up against. If it came to a choice between rocks and revelation, Hutton or Moses, there was hardly a contest – at least for some.

What these two little vignettes show is that seeing the significance of what is before us is not always obvious, or acceptable. This is particularly true if what is before us challenges beliefs or understandings of the world. However, Hutton was not alone. He was part of a broad tide of scholarship which had been rising and spreading inexorably across Europe for over the two centuries before the time of Hutton. It was called the *Scienza Nuova* – a term coined by the sixteenth-century Italian mathematician Niccolò Tartaglia – which became part of the European Enlightenment.[3] It was characterised by a new spirit of rational inquiry: empiricism – looking into the nature of things, observing, collecting, classifying, dissecting, demonstrating, theorising.[4] This was to become an increasingly distinctive, if not definitive, feature of modern European civilisation.

But at every new turn this spirit of inquiry found itself confronted and frustrated, as Hutton was, by traditional (usually ecclesiastical) authority. For two thousand years the authority of ancient Greek and

---

3. J. Israel, *Radical Enlightenment* (Oxford, 2001).
4. For a detailed evaluation of this period cf. B. Appleyard, *Understanding the Present: Science and the Soul of Modern Man* (Picador, 1992).

Roman writers – such as Aristotle, Galen, Ptolemy, Pliny, Dioscor-
ides – had become entwined with the even greater authority of the
Bible and Christian theology to create a revered body of knowledge
covering every aspect of life, which was deemed incontrovertible.
Encrusted around this edifice was a secondary world of fantasy and
myth, based on corrupted texts and pious legend, and credulously
digested tales from distant lands, inhabited by fabulous monsters:
leviathans, sirens, unicorns. For many, scholarship was simply the
reiteration of ancient learning from the classical world. Texts provided the ultimate reference for truth.[5]

As if all of this was not challenging enough for any rational en-
quirer, there was something more sinister to confront: the Inquisition. By this the mediating body of traditional learning – the
Catholic Church – had the means to crush any dissenting voices.
Though the case of Galileo has become iconic, it is by no means
exceptional. Even more interesting, and symptomatic, is the story of
the Fleming, Jan van Helmont, who was born in 1577, at the beginning of this new period of scientific endeavour. Though he described himself as a 'philosopher of fire' – presumably what we
would call an alchemist – one hesitates what exactly to call him,
which itself is indicative of the transitional cultural world he lived in.
He was what came to be called a 'natural philosopher' (the precursor
of the, as yet non-existent, 'scientist'), whose musings veered off into
a world of nature mysticism, magic and even charlatanry. Like his
contemporary John Dee, the Queen's Conjuror in the court of
Elizabeth I, he was constantly involved in 'experiments' in the natural
order that might give an insight into arcane workings of the mind of
God, but which could also be challenging to conventional wisdom.[6]

One such experiment concerned the investigation of the popular
belief that trees lived by 'eating' soil. With an alchemist's concern for
exact measurement and observation van Helmont weighed a tub of
soil and then a willow tree, which he watered for five years and then

---

5. The full story is given in D. Boorstin, *The Discoverers: A History of Man's Search to
   Know his World and Himself* (Phoenix, 1983).
6. B. Woolley, *The Queen's Conjuror: The Life and Magic of Dr. Dee* (Collins, 2001) for
   an insight into this fascinating transitional period between magic and science.

weighed again. As the weight of the soil remained the same (almost) he concluded that the vital element to plant life was water. Such an experiment is almost risible in its simplicity, yet its implications were momentous. Not only did it mark the beginning of the new science of botany, with the identification of the vascular system of plants, but it led van Helmont to reject the Aristotelian four-element theory – much as Galileo's experiments had led to his rejection of Aristotelian mechanics. That prompted van Helmont to return to the Ionian fount of the Greek and European scientific tradition, resurrecting Thales' concept of cosmic creation out of chaos. From this latter word he coined the term 'gas' to describe the primal atmosphere from whence all things came. All this from simple experimental observation.[7]

From such torturous roots the tree of modern scientific thinking began to arise. Perhaps even more significant were the circumstances in which the experimentation was done. Having already had one brush with the Inquisition, van Helmont did not relish a further one, which might well have been fatal. As a result all his work, like that of many similar minded people, was done in strictest secrecy and the results not published in his lifetime. In this he followed the example of that other precise observer of nature, Copernicus, whose meticulous recordings of planetary movement were also kept secret until after his death; though this did not prevent his posthumous exhumation and burning by the Inquisition.

If it is hard for us now to think that observing a plant grow is potentially both heretical and criminal, then this is indicative of how far we have travelled culturally over the last four centuries. However, still unresolved at the heart of our society and the larger context of what is called Western civilisation, are the tensions between religious belief and science, tradition and innovation. A popular view of this conflict, based in part on a reading of the influential sociologist Max Weber, is that the Protestant Reformation enabled the rise of indivi-

---

7. P. Strathern, *Mendeleyev's Dream: The Quest for the Elements* (Hamish Hamilton, 2000) for an account of the origins of modern chemistry.

dualism, unchaining enterprise and creative thinking from the oppressive power of Catholicism.[8] That this is most certainly naïve is illustrated by the story of James Hutton and innumerable other exploratory thinkers, for whom biblically based Protestantism could be equally oppressive.

Though we should not underestimate the destructive power of traditional religious authoritarianism – as can be seen from the decisive role this played in Muslim countries in bringing an end to the Golden Age of Islamic science[9] – what we can observe in European society is a more subtle process at work, which expressed itself in a profound paradox. On the one hand, Christianity provided the basis for the growth of a distinctive world view, characterised by a belief in a creator-God who was rational, consistent and benign; creation itself being seen as expressive of principles which were comprehensible.[10] This set of unique beliefs, which characterised the medieval world, led to an increasing interest in natural inquiry and gave scholasticism the confidence to search into nature for a rational vindication of faith. As the distinguished mathematician A.N. Whitehead wrote in his classic study of *Science and the Modern World*, 'faith in the possibility of science' was, for the development of modern scientific theory, 'an unconscious derivative from medieval theology.'[11]

In a more recent reflection on the dynamics of Western civilisation, *The Suicide of the West*, Richard Koch and Chris Smith point out that, 'From the thirteenth to the seventeenth centuries, virtually every important Western scientist was a Christian.'[12] That leads to the other arm of paradox: though carried out largely under the pretext of promoting Christian belief, and mostly by clerics, the new thinking of these proto-scientists was constantly frustrated not only by ecclesiastical authority but by inadequate paradigms of thought, often derived from the Bible; so much so that often no progress

8. M. Weber, *The Protestant Ethic and the Spirit of Capitalism* (Economy, 2012) and R. Tawney, *Religion and the Rise of Capitalism* (Pelican, 1969).
9. E. Masood, *Science and Islam: A History* (Icon, 2009) and J. Al-Kahlili, *Pathfinders: The Golden Age of Arabic Science* (Allen Lane, 2010).
10. P. Hodgson *Is Science Christian?* (Catholic Truth Society, 1978).
11. A. N. Whitehead, *Science and the Modern World* (Cambridge University Press, 1926).
12. R. Koch & C. Smith, *The Suicide of the West* (Continuum, 2006).

could be made until these paradigms were set aside. For example, it was only by setting aside the accepted biblical chronology of the Earth in favour of 'deep time' that Hutton's thought could move forward.[13]

Even so, progress was no straightforward matter, as can be seen from the life of the pioneering botanist, John Ray. Ray was himself an ordained minister who abandoned a promising career at Cambridge to become a Dissenter, refusing to subscribe to the Act of Uniformity with the established church. Henceforth he followed a solitary career researching and classifying plants. Though even that innocuous pursuit could be construed as meddling with things the Creator had simply made for his pleasure, Ray chose to see it as discerning the patterns that reflected the symmetry and orderliness of God's perfect mind, thereby becoming a defence of religion. In his most popular work, *The Wisdom of God Manifested in the Works of Creation*, he argued that whilst 'illiterate persons of the lowest Rank' need no proof of God as the world cannot make itself, 'There is no greater … Argument of the Existence of a Deity than the admirable Art and Wisdom that discovers itself in the mode and constitution, the order and disposition … of Heaven and Earth.'[14]

By collecting and ordering innumerable specimens of plants Ray contrived to identify and categorise their defining characteristics. This work of classification was a ground-breaking approach that contrasted with the contemporary alphabetical lists. Even more so was the word he coined to facilitate it: 'species' – simply derived from the Latin *specere,* 'to look at' or 'to see'. Literally, he was ordering what he

---

13. A radically different approach to the investigation of the natural world was taken in the Muslim world after the eleventh century and typified by it most influential exponent, al Ghazali, who simply dismissed its necessity on the basis that God could do whatever he wants so there was no such thing as a natural order. Such a view – called 'occasionalism' – was expounded in his famous work *The Incoherence of the Philosophers* (sometimes translated as *The Destruction of the Philosophers*), whose title really says it all and is a view which is still influential in the Muslim world, Cf. S. Weinberg, *To Understand the World* (Allen Lane, 2015), ch. 9. Though, to be fair, such anti-scientific views increasingly typify Christian fundamentalists in the USA.
14. K. Thomson, *The Watch on the Heath: Science and Religion before Darwin* (Harper, 2005).

could see. But this seminal scientific word and concept had implications of its own. Though Ray chose to emphasis the fixed distinctiveness of species, thus conforming with the fixed order of creation, there were other implicit possibilities. Where the proximity of similar species seemed to blend, it brought with it the possibility of 'chance collisions', which could modify the 'fixed' order. Ray denounced this 'ridiculous' possibility, but it was not long before nurserymen were exploiting it and hybridising species. This they did again in the greatest secrecy and under cover of darkness for fear of being denounced for 'playing God'.

But there were further new possibilities. In introducing his *Methodus Planatarum* Ray cautioned his readers that though he had not described all the species of plants, none would be left 'homeless' for all have a special place: 'Nature, as the saying goes, makes no jumps and passes from extreme to extreme only through a mean.' Together with this wonderful cornucopia of species went the implication of a carefully graded and integrated order of incomprehensible breadth and diversity, which also extended to other creatures. An even more potent implication lay embedded in this close association of species, one which would make possible a further idea: evolution.

Science seemed to carry a hidden potency of its own, opening up new prospects regardless of the author's intentions. Over time, with ever more experimentation, the divide between what might be believed and the implications of what was observed seemed to grow, a divide which could undermine the beliefs that initiated the process. Thus one was left with a dilemma: whether to pursue or abort one's studies. This can clearly be seen in the life of one of Ray's contemporaries, the Danish scientist Niels Stenson.[15] Stenson must surely go down as one of the most precocious yet conflicted geniuses of all time. Having identified the true nature of fossils and the process of fossilisation, his seminal studies of rock formation and stratification – which would lay the foundations for the future science of geology – were initially published in his famous *Prodromus* (Prologue), planned as the beginning of a much greater work, but never followed up.

---

15. A. Culter, *The Seashell on the Mountaintop: A Story of Science, Sainthood and the Humble Genius who Discovered a New History of the Earth* (Arrow, 2004) for a biography of Niels Stenson/Nicolaus Steno.

Instead, he converted to Catholicism, became a bishop, dropped all his scientific work, showing no further interest in it. A life of rigorous asceticism led to an early death. There is no doubt the implications of his observations and theories would not have been to the liking of the Inquisition and it seems he himself recoiled from their implications.

The geological baton Stenson dropped would be taken up by John Hutton. But the significance of Hutton and other natural philosophers, or proto-scientists, lay not just in the discovery of new physical processes. Of much greater significance was the implication that the process of observation had for the very nature of thought itself; it was no use trying to shoe-horn new knowledge into old conceptual categories. Darwin felicitously phrased the effect of thinking about geology as, 'it altered the tone of one's mind'. That knowledge itself could evolve was perhaps the most profound consequence of the *Scienza Nuova:* new facts need new thinking. In turn new thinking uncovered new facts. Science became a self-sustaining catalytic activity. As science writer Bryan Appleyard noted in his study of modern science and society, *Understanding the Present*, 'from the seventeenth century to our own day, our culture was to embrace novelty with accelerating intensity and formidable consequences. The need for innovation was born with science.'[16]

A whirlwind of innovation and change now engulfs the globe; the pursuit of novelty is a defining characteristic of modern 'scientific' societies, driving consumption. The pace of change is both momentous and breathtaking. The 'ridickulous' philosophies denounced by Ray have now become the orthodox paradigms of 'Atomick Atheists'. But older suspicions still remain; echoes of the drama of Copernicus and Galileo, van Helmont and Hutton still resonate, even the belligerent denial of scientific evidence is becoming increasingly popular as religious fundamentalist and neo-conservative thinkers cling to traditional authority as tenaciously as the inquisitors of old. Fortunately, they now lack their judicial power, but perhaps because of where we are now, we can better appreciate just how radical the humble disposition of people like James Hutton and John

---

16. Appleyard, *ibid.*

Ray really was: to look at what stands before us whilst setting aside previous preconceptions – not as easy as it might at first sound.

CHAPTER 5

Changing Time

How clocks changed our lives and created a secular world

One of my favourite pieces of spiritual reading has long been the opening passage of Jean-Pierre de Caussade's treatise, *Self-Abandonment to Divine Providence*, also known as *The Sacrament of the Present Moment*.[1] This classic text of eighteenth century Quietism urges not only an acceptance of what life throws at us – seen then from the perspective of a divinely preordained purpose – but also of our 'duty' to grasp the opportunities presented in the present moment. In passing he refers to, 'the hand of a clock which marks each moment of the hour' as the model for fixing our attention on the possibilities of 'each successive moment'.

It is an analogy which I have always found quite compelling. Each moment comes with its own potentialities and opportunities for good or bad. Each moment is unique and once passed it will never return – we live our lives moment by moment because we can do no other: things only happen in the present. But whatever one may think of this as a spiritual attitude, the interesting thing is that this analogy is closely dependent on, in fact defined by, technology. It was only by the eighteenth century that clocks were becoming so widely available as to become common household objects, made possible by sophisticated levels of craftsmanship. But it was not only the technology that is of interest. Even more significant was the effect it was having on society and people's lives.

Before the eighteenth century it was common to see life as part of a grand cosmic order, very much as de Caussade did, with everything in the heavens nicely ordered and harmonised. There were seven planets, seven days of the week, and seven daily times for prayer, which provided the basis of monastic ritual. It was also a moral order, as vividly depicted in Dante's *Divine Comedy*.

---

1. Jean-Pierre de Caussade, *Self-Abandonment to Divine Providence* (Fontana, 1972).

Unfortunately, this order had been disturbed, first by Copernicus and then even more aggressively by Galileo, opining that there were other heavenly bodies doing all sorts of strange things. Curiously, the more knowledge we have gained, the more confused things have become, and now we are not even quite sure how many planets there are, with 'planetesimals' and proto-planets constantly clamouring for our attention. For pre-modern societies such indeterminacy would have been unthinkable. Precise astrological conjecture was essential to guiding human actions – of what was propitious and what was not. Such conjecture could be a matter life and death, dependent not only on months or days but even hours and minutes – as with eclipses. Such obsessiveness was particularly true of Chinese society and it seems that the first recognisably mechanical clock of some sophistication was the Su Sung clock built at the end of the eleventh century with the intention of tracking minute changes in the cosmos – even if it was only to determine whether the emperor slept with the empress or one of his concubines.

It is unclear whether this invention prompted horological developments in Europe but in a book called *Heavenly Clockwork* by a group of Chinese scholars, led by the celebrated Sinologist Joseph Needham, they argued that it was. If so it was acquired and developed by the monasteries in Europe as a useful accessory for marking the hours of prayer essential to ritual. As they put it: 'The mechanical clock is nought but a fallen angel from the world of astronomy.'[2] No other group had such a pressing need for regular timekeeping, or the time and resources to pursue possibilities. Nor was any other group so engaged in all the technologies surrounding the production of clocks, such as metal-smelting, whose patron was the great Benedictine reformer, St. Dunstan.

There is a debate to be had as to whether the need for a highly synchronised society, such as a large medieval monastery, led to the invention of the clock or the introduction of the mechanical clock led to an interest in time-keeping. Either way, the first clocks were beginning to appear in the fourteenth century: by 1350 Richard of

---

2. Ying-Hsing, Sung. *Chinese Technology in the Seventeenth Century.* (Dover, 1997). Cf. also. J. Needham, *Science and Civilisation in China* (Cambridge University Press, 1954).

Wallingford was constructing a complex astronomical clock at the monastery of St. Albans and a clock tower was installed in Norwich cathedral. Soon this useful spiritual accessory was moving beyond the confines of the cloister to the market place. Increasingly complex mechanical clocks became a 'must have' for towns across Europe, vying to outdo each other with the number of gizmos attached to them.

As is so often the case with technology, the consequences of the appearance of the clock were more far-reaching than either antici-pated or obvious at first. The monasteries so embedded time into their social organisation that historian Alan Macfarlane suggested, in a sense they became 'a living clock, a kind of physical-social clock in their order.'[3] As this phenomenon moved into the market place, it slowly but surely began to impose the discipline of time on the popu-lace at large. Not only the sacred order but the secular order came to be increasingly characterised by time-keeping. In fact now, so over-bearing is the tyranny of the clock, that we not only have one on the market place tower or in the hallway of our house but we have one strapped to our wrist, so that we never escape. In our increasingly frenzied society not only every minute but every second counts.

Some historians have seen this development as a fundamental ele-ment in the creation and character of modern industrial society: as Sally Dugan wrote on *The Roots of the Industrial Revolution,* 'The regular rhythm of the demands of God was a foretaste of the more strident stroke of the Machine Age.'[4] Just as innumerable choirs of monks were once corralled by the chiming bell on the stroke of the hour, so centuries later, scores of workers were coerced through the mill gates by the factory whistle announcing work time. What started out for the sanctification of man ended with his dehumanisation into an automaton of production: the vocational allure of the sacred portals to heavenly bliss were, in time, replaced by the regimented compul-sion of industrialised life. Ultimately, it was a journey which led through the iron work gates of a hell where, in the sardonic motto of the Auschwitz labour camp, 'Work makes Free'. It was the clock that

---

3. A. Macfarlane, *The Savage Wars of Peace* (Blackwell, 1997).
4. S & D Duggan, *The Day the World Took Off: The Roots of the Industrial Revolution* (Channel 4 Books, 2000).

allowed the regulation of the work-force that made possible modern industrialised society, just as it made possible the synchronised time-tables of the railways which bound the new order together – and also delivered its human cargos to the death camps.

But this is not the only unforeseen consequence of the clock, nor even its most significant. One feature, if not the most distinctive, of Western society is the importance it attaches to the individual and individualism. It is an intriguing coincidence that the concept of the individual began to appear at the same time as clocks. In his recent study, *Inventing the Individual: The Origins of Western Liberalism,* Larry Siedentop writes, 'If we look at the word 'individual' in historical dictionaries of the English and French languages, we will find that it first became current in the fifteenth century.'[5]

Why this should be so is open to discussion. Siedentop opines that this is the outcome of a long prehistory of church teaching which emphasised both individual freedom and moral equivalence before God. The philosopher Michael Foucault noted the importance of monastic confessional practice and the private confession of sins that had helped to define the individual as a 'subject' by the thirteenth century.[6] By this time developments in canon law also led to a new understanding of social order and sovereignty based on the individual moral agent, which gradually undermined feudal social norms, introducing an unprecedented element of personal autonomy. This individualism was also reflected in the new wave of popular spirituality across Europe stressing 'innerness', which became the leitmotiv of German and Dutch mystics, as well as the followers of Wycliffe and Huss. Their fight for conviction rather than conformity harbingered the beginning of the individualism that characterises modern liberalism.

An accomplice of this seismic ontological change in understanding was the clock. With it time gradually became uncoupled from the

---

5. L. Siedentop, *Inventing the Individual: The Origins of Western Liberalism* (Allen Lane, 2014) Siedentop challenges the established view that the roots of Western individualism are to be found in the secular enlightenment of the seventeenth century and makes a convincing argument that its roots are much earlier, being deeply embedded in the preceding history of Christian Europe with the significance it ascribed to the individual as an autonomous moral agent.
6. M. Foucault, *The History of Sexuality,* vol. 2 (Penguin, 1984).

great cosmic order of inevitability and broken down into discrete units that could be personalised, as Lewis Mumford wrote in *Technics and Civilisation,* 'Time-keeping passed into time-serving and time-accounting and time-rationing.'[7] Individuals could begin to organise their day around their own needs, with public time for work and private 'time to oneself', as the phrase has it. As individual time pieces began to appear they gave people control over how they spent their time. The turning hand of the clock no longer pointed to the inevitability of Providence – as de Caussade would have it – but as a measure of time spent or time lost.

Cambridge historian Simon Schaffer thinks the growing awareness of personal time is critical to the creation of a new kind of European society: 'I see a very strong relationship, which emerges between the 1300s and the 1500s, between mechanical clocks and an individualisation or privatisation of time.'[8] For this new development it is important to look away from the monastic kind of coordinated world to one in which individuals could arrange meetings, plan what to do and measure what others were doing. Freedom to arrange one's affairs and go about one's business began to underpin a new kind of secular order or state, which is implicitly neutral and democratic.[9] As the influence of the clock spread it became a prod to personal achievement and productivity; 'Eternity ceased gradually to serve as the measure and focus of human actions.' In time, personalised time became the concomitant of personal freedom.

Again one wonders if it is just a coincidence that, contemporary with the appearance of the word 'individual' in the fifteenth century,

---

7. Quoted in Duggan, *ibid.* p. 108.
8. Quoted in Duggan *ibid.* p. 107.
9. Siedentop argues that the new image of society as an association of individuals – a state – began to emerge in the fifteenth century as an unintended consequence of feudal monarchies with their centralising regimes: 'The monarchs not only created states, but also the foundation for a "public" or "national" opinion.' P. 346. The beginnings of this process were to be found in the Investiture Controversy of the eleventh century, the paradoxical outcome of which was that, 'The Emperor as Emperor was now thrust out of the Church, and the Empire became a secular reality.' Cf. C. Davis. *Religion and the Making of Society* (Cambridge, 1994), p.3. Soon monarchs were having their 'divine right' challenged by individuals, as with King John and the imposition of the Magna Carta in 1215, the seminal document of modern society.

the new word 'state' also appeared. Siedentop thinks not, for 'It was through the creation of states that the individual was invented as the primary or organising social role.'[10] New ways of being were the corollary to a new understanding of the state and the fundamental feature of modern society began to emerge: an individualistic society – a model in which the individual rather than the family, clan or caste is increasingly the basic social unit.

If there is a link between the clock and a new sense of individuality and society, perhaps one can check this by cross-referencing to what was happening in other, non-Western, cultures of the same period. Curiously, in China no public clocks were built in towns. This is a bit of a puzzle as craftsmen certainly had the capability to build them and there was a demand for them, as Matteo Ricci cleverly anticipated in his epochal mission to China.[11] The emperor was more intrigued by the clocks he brought than by anything else. An explanation is perhaps to be found in the autocratic nature of the state: time, like everything else, was a commodity owned by the emperor and solely for his benefit. Oddly, in the Forbidden City clocks struck the hours only at night but this was so that those seeking an imperial audience could time their passage through the layers of officialdom and ensure that the emperor was not kept waiting. Nothing else mattered – not much concession to individual rights here.

Similarly, in Islamic states there were no public clocks until the nineteenth century, when one was built in Istanbul. Across the centuries European travellers, like Jean Chardin in 1674, often noted there were 'neither clocks nor watches.'[12] This is doubly surprising as there was both a distinguished tradition of sophisticated astronomical devices in the Islamic world, which far surpassed those of Europe, and there was also the common practice of dividing the day into times of prayer, reminiscent of the monastic world of Europe. An ambassador of Charles V journeying to the Ottoman capital in 1554 remarked on the annoyance caused by never knowing when to

---

10. Siedentop, *ibid.* p. 347.
11. V.Cronin, *The Wise Man from the West* (Fount, 1984).
12. Quoted in B. Lewis, *What Went Wrong? The Clash between Islam and Modernity* (Weidenfeld & Nicolson, 2002).

get up, for 'at night there is nothing to mark the time.' He also perceived the reason for this state of affairs: 'They think that the authority of their muezzins and their ancient rites would suffer diminution.'[13] Submission – the very meaning of the word Islam – was what was required, not individuality.

Neither of these cultures had much use for clocks nor individualism. Perhaps part of the explanation for the difference between cultures relates to their geographical location. Whilst Islamic lands are generally near the equator, where the days are more equitable and the sun a sufficiently reliable guide to the time, in more northerly European latitudes the length of day varies enormously with the seasons and so necessitates some other means of telling the time. The clock provided a solution to this problem but in doing so subtly uncoupled the link between society and its heavenly context.

Another part of the explanation for the cultural contrast was that authoritarian and theocratic states had space neither for individuality nor the individual keepers of time, clocks. In his post-9/11 reflection on the clash between Islam and Modernity, *What Went Wrong?* the distinguished scholar of Near Eastern studies, Bernard Lewis, noted the fundamental social change that arose from the role of technology. As with clocks so with that other potentially threatening agent of individual thought and social change, the printing press: there was no place for these in a society where a sacred domain had to be protected and conformity was expected.[14]

It is only when one considers in detail the subtle consequences of technological innovation – often undetected and unintended – that their significance becomes apparent in the process of secularisation. Up until the time of Newton there was no contradiction between theology and science, and an understanding of time was deemed crucial to understanding the Bible. As Simon Schaffer says, 'Newton and his ilk were able to make their fantastically ingenious calculations about time by looking at chronology sequences and astronomical events mentioned by previous civilisations and correlating them to events mentioned in the Bible.'[15] By analysing classical and biblical

13. Lewis, *ibid.* p. 117.
14. Lewis, *ibid.*
15. G. Grant, *Time's Change* (Cambridge Alumni Magazine, 2008, no. 54).

texts as well as ancient Babylonian and Chinese data, gradually firm data ranges for life, mirroring but independent of the Bible, were constructed. Though originally people didn't like tinkering with God's timepiece, the universe, in time an autonomous way of viewing it began to emerge. Interestingly the man most accredited with disturbing the traditional view of the heavens, Galileo, also saw the pendulum as the means to create an accurate and autonomous time piece. As a result society began to view itself and the world in a different, secular way.

This is part of the theme taken up by Terry Eagleton in his latest work, *Culture and the Death of God:* that modern societies have become faithless by their very nature.[16] In this thesis, scientific developments and the rise of an industrial middle class have created a radically new way of life, which is both artificial and fundamentally irreligious in that it is 'totally alien to the category of the sacred.' Though he lists a host of secularising factors such as science, technology, education and social mobility that have helped create modern society, he does not mention perhaps the most potent of all – time, and the new sort of society that the clock helped to create.

By the end of the eighteenth century, clocks were poised to make their greatest contribution yet to changing the way we live, though again surreptitiously. By this time European clockmakers had become masters in the transmission and control of motion through complex gearing systems and escape mechanisms. Now this technology could be scaled up and harnessed to the newly discovered steam power, to provide automated machines on a much larger scale. These were the machines that created the Industrial Revolution which changed the world and the way we live. As Lewis Mumford wrote, with characteristic incisiveness, 'The clock, not the steam engine, is the key machine of the modern industrial age. For every phase of its development the clock is both the outstanding fact and typical symbol of the machine.'[17] The mechanised time-keeper now began to create a mechanised society.

It is coordinated mechanical time that has made the modern world possible. Time zones span the world so that time in any one

---

16. T. Eagleton, *Culture and the Death of God* (Yale, 2014).
17. Quoted in Duggan, *ibid.*

place is related to every other place. Our computers are all set according to one master clock (at the US Naval Institute, Washington, DC), now no longer mechanical but atomic, providing us all with International Atomic Time, so precise that its variance is only a matter of seconds over billions of years. It operates regardless of belief or culture and, whether we recognise it or not, we are all to some extent in its thrall. Our financial markets, travels details, sat-navs, PCs and every detail of our lives are time-related to enable us to function as one global society. Whatever any individual is doing at any one place or point of time can be coordinated with any other individual anywhere in the world. The clock has made time the one all-pervading feature of the secular world of modernity binding together a global community.

Our understanding of space and time, or Einsteinian 'space-time', has now been transformed, and with it our understanding of ourselves. Though the theologian William Paley once tried to make a case for 'the Divine Watchmaker', we now understand the cosmos to be the product of self-organising evolutionary forces, the work, if anything, of *The Blind Watchmaker*, as Richard Dawkins rather facetiously entitled his well-known work. Yet as we gaze out into the depths of space, we also understand that we are looking back in time, even to the very beginning of everything. Curiously, everything is present – there is no time, only the ever present moment.

This is a view not too distant from that of de Caussade, with which I began this reflection, a mystical view worthy of contemplation. Though our *milieu* is now radically changed and we may no longer see the present moment as the agent of providential design, we can certainly agree that it is of paramount importance. Though we may no longer hear the slow, rhythmic ticking of the clock – now replaced by a barely perceptible electronic hum – the moving hands on the clock face may still prompt us to useful meditation on how, in time, the sacred world gave rise to secular modernity, without us ever really noticing.

CHAPTER 6

What's Become of Us?

The advent and nature of post-biblical thinking

Perhaps you missed the celebrations for the six thousandth anniversary of the universe, on 23rd October 2004. It seems to have been a rather muted affair, even among the resurgent evangelical groups in America who hold to a literal reading of the Bible. True, the Bible does not actually mention a specific date, but it has long been held that the text holds clues and, as is the case in such matters, revelation is by way of code.

Across the centuries great minds have grappled with decoding the sacred text: the Venerable Bede, for example, computed a date of 3952 BC for the beginning of things. But it was not until 1655 that the great Hebrew scholar and Vice-Chancellor of Cambridge University, John Lightfoot, gave the definitive and widely accepted date for the moment of creation. It was now clear that on 23rd October 4004 BC at nine o'clock in the morning that, 'Heaven and Earth, centre and circumference, were created all together, in the same instant, and clouds full of water.' Archbishop Ussher agreed but actually added up his dates wrong.[1]

A generation later it occurred to another Cambridge cleric and scholar, Thomas Burnet, whilst crossing the Alps, that the chaotic features of the mountains had not been created *ab origine* by God but were the after-effects of the Flood: mountains were, in effect, gigantic reminders of humanity's sinfulness. If this were so it implied the Earth was subject to periodic change. Burnet set out his view that the Earth had a history (guided of course by the Creator) in his book

---

1. For general background: H. Brown, *The Wisdom of Science: Its Relevance to Culture and Religion* (Cambridge, 1986) also D. Boorstin, *The Discoverers: A History of Man's Search to Know His World and Himself* (Phoenix, 1983).

The Sacred Theory of the Earth (1684). It was a 'theory' which immediately provoked outrage, as it seemed to suggest a defect in the original design.[2] Though Burnet's career was ruined by his application of scripture and counter-doctrinal ideas, a new dimension had been introduced into the discussion about Creation – change.

For change to work it needed time. That geological time was endless, with 'no vestige of a beginning – no prospect of an end', is an idea we owe to Edinburgh proto-scientist James Hutton (1726-1797). The idea was also taken up by a precocious French natural historian, Count Georges Buffon (1707-88), who, whilst realising the need for time in creation, was clever enough to evade a direct challenge to the established Catholic orthodoxy, risking ruin and imprisonment, by proposing that the 'days' of creation might be a metaphor for longer periods of time. In public Buffon was suggesting perhaps tens of thousands of years. In private he was thinking something altogether more blasphemous: in notes discovered posthumously was scribbled a figure of several billion years. This is what we now call 'deep time'.

The growing interest in fossils seemed to provide an alternative to the biblical record of events. But all this was speculation: no one had any definite dates of anything from ancient times other than what the Bible recorded. Enter the Egyptologist, Jean-Francois Champollion (1790-1832). His deciphering of the ancient hieroglyphs and subsequent trip to Egypt in 1822 to study the ancient monuments revealed a world which could be dated independently of the Bible, for the record of the pharaohs stretched beyond 3,000 BC. This radical claim obviously had serious and subversive implications for biblical chronology, which provoked the wrath of both Church and state. In the face of the resurgent traditionalism of the Bourbons – reminiscent of the neo-conservatism of today – Champollion narrowly avoided imprisonment.[3]

But there was worse to come. Fossil hunters, such as Gideon Mantell (1790-1852) in Sussex, were discovering evidence of whole

2. The details of this controversy are discussed by another Cambridge scholar R. Macfarlane, *Mountains of the Mind* (Granta, 2003).
3. L & R Adkins, *The Keys of Egypt: The Race to Read the Hieroglyphs* (Harper Collins, 2001).

worlds inhabited by creatures whose natures beggared belief. This former creation, in which horrific carnage was part of daily life, seemed inexplicable in terms of traditional biblical theodicy: why would God create such hideous monsters? The responses swung from denial to the view that these were Satan's creatures, 'armed with the virility of Evil... a teeming Spawn fitted for the lowest abysm of Chaos.' Such 'dinosaurs' (demon lizards) challenged not only the order of creation but the very nature of the creator who had designed it. The eminent Oxford geologist Reverend William Buckland eventually had to accept that the carnivorous carnage was 'inconsistent with a Creation founded in Benevolence', but recognition of the inconsistency no doubt had a part in causing his mental breakdown.[4]

What natural theology did do was to provide early scientists with the incentive and a metaphysical justification for their research, as geologist Charles Gillispie has pointed out, 'everyone agreed natural history must devote itself to exhibiting evidence of divine design and material Providence.'[5] So the search for evidence of natural phenomena expanded and provided the background to the famous voyage of Charles Darwin. But the results were not always reassuring, as in the case of the Galapagos islands. For the 'God of Galapagos' did not seem to be a loving God who cared about his productions but one who was careless, wasteful, indifferent, almost diabolical: 'certainly not the sort of God to whom anyone would be inclined to pray.'[6]

As intelligent beings we constantly seeks the signs of intelligibility imprinted in the universe. Either by divination or experimentation we are driven to discern what this intelligent design may be. With the discovery of deep space in the twentieth century, thanks to the work of Edwin Hubble (identifying an expanding universe), and later revelations from the Hubble space telescope, there is every reason to reject this assumption of intelligibility and design. What the universe does reveal is that not only does it have a vast and violent history but that it is much more mysterious and unintelligible than we ever had

---

4. D. Cadbury, *The Dinosaur Hunters* (Fourth Estate, 2000).
5. Quoted in E. Larson, *Evolution's Workshop: God and Science on the Galapagos Islands* (Penguin, 2002).
6. Larson, *ibid.*

reason to believe. It would seem that in the dark matter which comprises perhaps 95% of the universe intelligibility ceases, whilst black holes even lead to alternative universes.[7]

Indeed, one of the most paradoxical results of our growing knowledge is, as the Astronomer Royal, Martin Rees, pointed out, our minds have now reached the threshold of recognising their own incapacity: 'The micro-structure of empty space could be far too complex for unaided human brains to grasp.'[8] It seems that of necessity much of reality is beyond the range of our sensory receptors. Our senses provide limits to act as a safety valve for the mind, to protect it from being overloaded with information. What the brain does remarkably well is to compress information into algorithms – patterns of recognition. But these are not discovered – as the ancients thought – they are created, by us: to some extent what we are seeing is a product of what we are thinking or looking for. Science forces us to think in very 'unnatural' or counter-intuitive ways: one may stand and watch the sun 'moving' across the heavens only to realise that really it is the other way round. Not only is the universe more mysterious than we know, it is more mysterious than we *can* know.

Of course it is possible to postulate a Higher Intelligence which overrides all such limitations. The reason to reject such a *deus ex machina* is from the evidence of the universe we do know, in particular the reality of catastrophe. The Boxing Day tsunami of 2004, for example, reminded us of the difficulties of relating the idea of benign creation with natural catastrophes: the Archbishop of Canterbury spoke of the event as a test of people's faith; in Indonesia mullahs spoke of a punishment for sin (like girls riding pavilion passengers on boys' motor scooters or wearing incorrect dress). Unless one wants to suggest that, like the Flood, it is a punishment for sin, catastrophic change implies not so much a defect in design as no design at all, which, as the critics of Burnet pointed out, undermines the conventional understanding of scripture.

The rebirth of catastrophism in the 1970s came with the realisation that after 180 million years the 'demonic' dinosaurs were all

---

7. J. Barrow, *The Book of Universes* (Bodley Head, 2011).
8. M. Rees, *Our Final Century* (Heinemann, 2003).

but exterminated by a random meteorite strike. Other such random events seemed to abound in the story of the Earth, such as the 'oxygen holocaust', in which the original hydrogen-loving cells were destroyed over the period of a billion years by the oxygen they released.[9] The sheer scale of past extinctions has only recently become apparent and we now know that 99% of all past species have become extinct.[10] The mindless destruction of mindless creatures is itself a mindless act.

The discovery of deep time and deep space challenged pivotal assumptions of biblical thinking – that there is a beginning; a stable order; an intelligible design and benevolent purpose. It seemed that the biblical paradigm was not just defective, but fundamentally flawed. It is difficult for us to understand how drastically the discovery of time and change shook the foundations of the nineteenth-century world view, creating a climate of doubt and disbelief in the previously established Christian orthodoxy. Though much is made of the controversy over evolution in relation to previous biblical orthodoxy, far more disturbing from a creationist point of view is the catastrophe of extinction, for from the perspective of creationism the creation of species merely for destruction is pointless.

Still further challenges have come with the advent of what we may call deep life – the discovery of the genetic basis of life. Though we generally assume we know what life is, no one has ever been able to give it a credible definition, other than that it is an aspect of the universe.[11] If we cannot say what life is, then it becomes pointless asking when it began let alone how we should regard it. To the astrophysicist Fred Hoyle, 'our' sort of carbon-based life is a feature of the time and place in the universe we now inhabit, and where key

9. N. Lane, *Oxygen: The Molecule that made the World* (Oxford, 2002). Also, B. Swimme & T. Berry, *The Universe Story* (Arkana/Penguin, 1992) for a graphic account of the unfolding of the cosmos and the Earth's story, also now made into a film.
10. R. Leaky & R. Lewin, *The Sixth Extinction* (Weidenfeld & Nicolson, 1996).
11. F. Dyson, *Infinite in All Directions: The Gifford Lectures 1985* (Penguin, 1988). He writes, 'The question, at which point along that sequence of events we draw the line between non-living and living, is not a scientific question. The line between living and non-living at the beginning of evolution is arbitrary… the task of science is not to define the exact position of the line but to understand how it came to be crossed.' P.54.

elements have had the time to form from the ashes of long dead stars – we are star dust![12]

The best shot at penetrating the mystery of 'What is Life?' came from a professor of theoretical physics in 1944. In a book of that name Erwin Schrodinger, who had previously worked out the mathematical basis of quantum mechanics, postulated a molecular basis for genes, in which the number of atoms and energy levels would create mutations analogous to those which existed in quantum physics.[13] From this insight has come our understanding of the genetic component of our planetary life. In this saga, the evolution of the cell has been the decisive step, in comparison with which everything else pales into insignificance. In the tree of life all the great 'domains' are microbial, with the multicellular organisms (like humans) occupying a very small and insignificant space in the grand spectacle of things.

Traditionally, as Richard Dawkins writes in his expansive genealogy of life, *The Ancestor's Tale*, the story of life has generally been told from the point of view of the 'big animals – us.'[14] But this is an entirely false perspective. In fact a piece of yeast or an amoeba is scarcely distinguishable from a human when viewed from the perspective of bacteria. We are but a slight variation on a theme which has been unfolding for a mere 500 million years, or since what is termed the Cambrian explosion of animal life, after which things become decidedly repetitive.[15] Though to us the variation seems vast, it is insignificant in relation to bacterial versatility, in comparison with which Dawkins says rather cynically, 'we are bacterial froth.' So much for the idea of fixed species.

---

12. L. Smolin, *The Life of the Cosmos* (Phoenix, 1997) Perhaps the greatest change in modern cosmology is the recognition that the cosmos does in fact have a life; that it is not a static entity of which we are a part, but that we are a product of a process of cosmogenesis.

13. E. Schrödinger, *What is Life?* (Cambridge, 1944).

14. R. Dawkins, *The Ancestor's Tale: A Pilgrimage to the Dawn of Life* (Phoenix, 2004).

15. N. Shubin, *Your Inner Fish* (Penguin, 2008) This curiously titled book tells the amazing story of how our whole anatomy has developed from the fish that first colonised the land 375 million years ago.

The new sense of deep life, a vast interconnected web of species some four billion years in the making, challenges the traditional biblical understanding of man as the 'lord of all he purveys'. This had its roots in the biblical belief of 'Adamite exceptionalism', that humanity only existed once,[16] and then in clear distinction from other animals, over which he has 'stewardship'. Like other 'clear distinctions' in the Bible – between clean and unclean, male and female, good and evil – they find little or no basis in reality as we now know it. Rather than helping us to understand who we are, they obscure our origins and the fact that the animals not only brought us to where we are but made us what we are. For the evolutionary biologist and palaeontologist Simon Conway Morris, the condescension we have towards birds and animals is tragic: 'We didn't, you know, get here on our own merits.'[17] For ecologist and Roman Catholic priest Thomas Berry we must now acknowledge, 'that nature has a prior stewardship over us.'[18] Our self-understanding is inextricably linked to our animal past: we're all animals now.

This is the basis of evolutionary psychology, which enables contemporary philosophers like Peter Singer not only to denounce the prejudice of 'speciesism' but to promote the novel concept of animal rights. For thinkers like Singer evolution explains the deepest characteristics of human behaviour, giving a different context to the discussion of morality: morally right action is about giving as many of us as possible what we want and need. Such 'preference utilitarianism', as it is called, contrasts to the apodictic morality of the Bible, which is blamed for a catastrophic disregard for animal life and the environment. As Singer says, 'In the West, we have been dominated by a single tradition for 2,000 years. Now that whole tradition, the

---

16. It is now clear that at the end of the Ice Age, c.15,000 BCE there were at least five hominid groups in different parts of the world, interacting and probably interbreeding, of which one was *homo sapiens*. At least a few percent of our genes are now known to come from Neanderthals. Cf. A. Roberts, *Evolution: the Human Story* (DK, 2012).
17. S. Conway Morris, *Rethinking Evolution* (Cambridge Alumni Magazine, 2012, no. 65).
18. T. Berry, *Select Writings on the Earth Community* (Orbis, 2014) p. 107.

whole edifice of Judaeo-Christian morality, is terminally ill...when morality shifts, people get confused and angry and disgusted.'[19]

The erosion of the credibility of biblical thinking and the assumptions on which it is based has also been accompanied by a re-evaluation of the integrity of the Bible itself. Biblical archaeology has not only increasingly come to question the accuracy of what it records but the status of the work as a whole.[20] From being seen as a prism through which to view the world, and a standard of judgement, it is now regarded as an artefact that was very much the product of its own limited world.

Yet the problem for the modern world is that the realm of objective or empirical knowledge which has replaced it seems even more unsatisfactory to the human spirit. In an influential work on the philosophical implications of the new understanding of life, aptly entitled *Chance and Necessity*,[21] the great French biologist and Nobel laureate, Jacques Monod, synthesised the insights of biology since Schrödinger, which showed that life was essentially a physical and mathematical phenomenon. Evolution can only take place because, although nucleic acids reproduce themselves exactly, accidental mistakes produce mutations. In this scenario the universe was an accident and life a mistake.

Confronted with this bleak view, Monod recognised the dreadful consequences for modern societies. These have become dependent on science like an addict on his drug, yet the material benefits of science have become detached from 'value-systems devastated by knowledge', but to which they still try to refer for guidance. No wonder Monod noted that many distinguished minds could not accept this state of affairs. Perhaps the current surge in neo-conservatism is evidence of this: it is simpler to believe old myths,

---

19. P. Singer, *Practical Ethics* (Cambridge, 1993).
20. I. Finkelstein & N Silberman, *The Bible Unearthed: Archaeology's New Vision of Ancient Israel and the Origin of its Sacred Texts* (Free Press, 2001). Ironically, the Jewish claim to Israel on the basis of biblical evidence has been undermined by the biblical archaeology intended to support it: key events such as the Exodus, the Conquest of Canaan, the Davidic Kingdom, Solomon's Temple are almost entirely fictitious and certainly never happened in the way portrayed in the Bible.
21. J. Monod, *Chance and Necessity* (Penguin, 1997).

just as it is to say that each day the sun rises and sets on our world, even though we know or suspect it to be false. Some now chose to ignore the evidence altogether: any myth is better than none. Such is the mentality at the heart of the new fundamentalisms, now possessing so many as they search for a spiritual anchor: the market for 'spirituality' has never been greater.

In his latest exploration of current spirituality, opaquely entitled *Looking into the Distance*, Bishop Richard Holloway notes that, 'What is now left of the explanatory use of God to account for the organised intricacies of planet Earth has retreated to one of the last frontiers of human knowledge, which is the human mind.'[22] It is here we may locate the fourth decisive 'depth' of modernity, the self.

The emergence of the modern sense of an individuated self is a process that is seen to have taken place in Europe after the fourteenth century.[23] The Reformation emphasis on individual salvation furthered this development and it is now a commonplace to see Shakespeare's works as reflecting the radical change in understanding human identity as an autonomous self.[24] A further critical step in this process was taken by the Oxford scholar Thomas Willis, whose seminal work, *Two Discourses on the Soul of Brutes,* from 1670, lays claim to be the foundation of the new science of neurology. The fact that the title indicates the work to be about animals (mainly dogs) reflects the taboo on investigating humans (other than in the form of cadavers) but Willis was proposing a radically new 'psychology' or doctrine of the soul, based on chemical spirits travelling along pathways through the brain into the nervous system.[25] In locating the source of action and behaviour in the functioning of the brain, Willis was taking the perilous step of challenging over two millennia of classical and Christian teaching.

---

22. R. Holloway, *Looking into the Distance: The Human Search for Meaning* (Canongate, 2004).
23. L. Siedentop, *Inventing the Individual: The Origins of Western Liberalism* (Allen Lane, 2014). He notes the word 'individual' enters English and French diction in the fifteenth century. P.347.
24. H. Bloom, *Shakespeare: The Invention of the Human* (Fourth Estate, 1998).
25. C. Zimmer. *Soul made Flesh: The Discovery of the Brain – and How it Changed the World* (Arrow, 2005).

Though the Bible saw the soul as simply life itself, residing in the blood and disappearing at death, the early church fathers sought an understanding of the soul as something immortal, that was given by God and survived death, for which they found support in the work of the Greek physician Galen. For him the soul was a vital, animating spirit which pulsated through the ventricles of the body; the body merely provided the physical residence for a spiritual substance, some 'thing' we were given and which we were called upon to save.[26] What Willis was doing was identifying an autonomous 'self' in the functioning of the brain, which was the source of consciousness. It is interesting to note that his work coincided with the growth of religious movements associated with pietism across Europe, emphasising inner experience and 'illumination'. To the Reformation cry of 'God alone', modernity now answered, 'Man alone'.

Since then a new and deeper sense of self has emerged as a hallmark of modernity. In the great Romantic transformation of the nineteenth century we see how the natural imagination replaced the supernatural in the poetic consciousness, thereby secularising theological concepts. For writers such as Wordsworth, Coleridge and Blake the supernatural became relocated into states of mind.[27] More recently, developments in neuroscience[28] have shown how deeply rooted 'states of mind' are within the evolutionary structure of the brain. As Holloway cogently notes, 'The mind is not some sort of self-existent ghost that temporarily inhabits our flesh; it is a way of describing how the brain expresses our bodies.'[29]

---

26. This is still a common view, as Cardinal Heenan once famously replied to a question on what was the purpose of life: 'To save my soul.' Confusingly, 'substance' is a word that has so completely changed in meaning since its usage by medieval scholastics that it now means almost the exact opposite of what they meant. The word 'soul' survives as a metaphor without relating to any reality: what Lloyd Geering called a frozen metaphor from a now obsolete world view.

27. M. Abrams, *Natural Supernaturalism: Tradition and Revolution in Romantic Literature* (Norton, 1971).

28. V. Ramachandra, *Phantoms in the Brain* (Fourth Estate, 1999), particularly ch. 9: 'God and the Limbic System', where he speculates, 'Maybe when the brain reaches a critical mass, new and unforeseen traits, properties that were not specifically chosen by natural selection, emerge.'

29. Holloway, *ibid.*

It was Freud's nephew, Edward Bernays (the founder of public relations) who recognised the potential for business in linking marketing to consumers' primitive, irrational drives – with immense success. Recently a senior marketing manager for Ford's attributed the immense success of SUVs to their appeal to our 'reptilian instincts' – bigger, stronger, faster ensures survival. The traditional appeal of reason and idealism has been undermined by what Robert Reich, a former Clinton advisor, termed 'the Freudian assumption' that our rational selves are 'little corks bobbing around on this great sea of hopes and fears and desires.' Politicians and demagogues also realised the potential here – with devastating consequences throughout the century.

Through the discovery of the true nature of deep time, deep space, deep life and the deep self, Western culture has gradually moved on beyond the paradigms of biblical thought. Its ancient myths now seem too small. Where they are retained they cramp the mind and obscure the truth, as can be seen even in the colossi of modern thought, such as Newton and Einstein: both held strong *a priori* views of divine agency, the former to ensure the absolute nature of space and time, the latter to ensure that the universe was not subject to chance unpredictability, that God did not 'play dice'. The contrary has been proved true for both: the intelligibility of the world has no longer a necessary link with God or religion, and reaches further than any theological special pleading. As the early geologists found, tinkering with these ancient assumptions is no help to enlightenment; there comes a point when new paradigms are needed.

This fills many with horror, that having renounced any higher purpose, humanity will relapse into carnivorous savagery. The resurgence of traditionalist beliefs in the USA is a clear expression of these fears and disillusionment with liberalism. They may also be the expression of confusion that arises from the very complexity and profundity of modern thought. Richard Rorty usefully distinguished the transition from the Aristotelian 'thing-nature' model of explanation, which lasted up to modern times, with a 'law-event' model of vastly greater reach.[30] People seem happier with tangible 'things': the more 'unobservables' (such as force, acceleration, quanta) science

---

30. R. Rorty, *Philosophy and Social Hope* (Penguin, 1999).

posits the less relevant they seem. Perhaps the creationist mantra that 'evolution is a theory not a fact' is one expression of this; to which the obvious riposte is that facts are meaningless without a theory, or higher level interpretive meaning.

It is interesting that Richard Holloway should subtitle his latest study of contemporary spirituality, *The Human Search for Meaning*.[31] Like Hamlet, humanity has journeyed to the edge of the abyss and, peering over, now stares into the Void – a place empty of meaning. As Holloway observes, this state is counter to our normal needs and desires: we want answers, explanations, explanatory systems – above all, something to look forward to. 'We are always waiting *for* something, which we anticipate patiently or impatiently.' Then, in a profound observation, which penetrates to the spiritual heart of modernity, he notes, 'For those of us who are living in the absence of God, waiting is not anticipatory; waiting is its own meaning, it is a permanent state of unknowing.'

And this is the point to which post-biblical thinking has led: we have come to the knowledge that the mysteries and complexity of the universe will forever lie beyond our comprehension. In fact, it was always a breathtaking illusion that it could ever be other than this: that a species of primate, which evolved in a particular environment on one small planet of one insignificant solar system, with restricted brain functions and only five limited senses, could ever imagine that it somehow knew and could judge all things with a magisterial rationality, is surely the greatest self-delusion of all. Mystics have always known this, though it was Nietzsche who put it most concisely: 'In some remote corner of the universe there was once a star on which clever animals invented knowledge. It was the most arrogant and mendacious moment of "universal history".'[32]

So we are condemned to do what humans find most difficult: to live in the present moment. Simply to be, with deference, in the presence of the world and the network of relations that surrounds us. By acting positively towards others through love and creativity we introduce value into our world. Like happiness, meaning is not

---

31. R. Holloway, *ibid.*
32. Quoted in D. Robinson, *Nietzsche and Postmodernism* (Icon, 1999) p.14.

something 'out there' we can decode or strive for, it is the consequence of our own attitude to others. When we look back over evolution's history, we see a drama that is savage, cruel, merciless and indifferent. Now for the first time intelligence (our intelligence) is able to act otherwise. We can assess the consequences of our actions and take ameliorative action: we can pity, care and be merciful (if we so choose). At a genetic level even in the random play of chance, which has always selected from the chaos of nature, we can now intervene for the good, something man always imagined his gods should do.

This also is the heart of beatitude, to live for the momentary good: 'consider the lilies of the field...' or as Nietzsche would have put it, 'be faithful to the Earth.' Long after we have destroyed the great animal species, and we ourselves have been destroyed, the basic structure of life will remain unchanged. The world will go on, perhaps to produce other intelligent species, who will look back on our colossal arrogance and stupidity, much as we look back on the dinosaurs.

II

LOOKING FORWARD

CHAPTER 7

What it Means to be Modern

The origins and future of a medieval idea

'Modern' is a word in constant use to describe our world and way of life. Yet, when we pause to inquire what this word actually means, it seems to disintegrate under scrutiny, very much as did the two very modern looking tower blocks of the World Trade Centre on 9/11. Everyone agreed that this was not just an attack on a building but on the whole modern way of life and the values that it represented. But attack by whom? This was not initially clear but a culprit was soon identified in 'international terrorism'. The only trouble is that when we come to ask what is 'terrorism' – itself a distinctive feature of modernity – we are back with the same problem: not even the finest diplomatic minds of the UN can agree a definition.

The most likely looking culprit seemed to be Islamist extremists. Here we have something that definitely looks 'non-modern', with a fundamentalist dedication to tradition which seems to be 'pre-modern', even medieval. Yet here is another curious thing: the very word 'modern' is medieval. It comes from a Latin word *'modo'*, which means 'just now', and amongst its first uses was to describe a breathtaking new kind of church architecture which first appeared in twelfth century France, the abbey of St Denis in Paris – the Twin Towers of its day.[1] We now call this kind of architecture 'Gothic'. But this is quite a modern word, which only appeared in the eighteenth century to describe the traditionalist reaction against the classical style that was then seen as modern. So that makes things even more confusing.

On the other hand, perhaps it is not so much Islamist fundamentalism as religion in general that is to be contrasted with what it

---

1. R. Appignanesi & C. Garratt, *Postmodernism* (Icon, 1995). By the fourteenth century the popular new secular spirituality was being referred to as the *Devotio Moderna*. Clergy not belonging to a religious order were regarded as 'secular', i.e. in the world.

is to be modern. This was certainly the case in the thinking of the Roman Catholic Church up until the middle of the twentieth century and the Second Vatican Council: 'modernism' was a catch-all term for everything that was held anathema, or 'contrary to the faith'. A famous and excoriating denunciation of the 'medievalism' of the church written at the beginning of the century by a famous Jesuit scholar, George Tyrrell, earned him simultaneously excommunication and vilification as the 'arch-modernist'.[2]

The most revolutionary document of the Vatican Council is often held to be *Gaudium et Spes* – usually translated into English as 'The Church in the Modern World' – which sought to break out from the paralysing state of fear and paranoia of modernity that had come to characterise the church: as Cardinal König said, it had to stop 'looking with fear on everything new in history.' But in fact, the English translation of the title of this revolutionary document is itself both interestingly indicative and misleading, because it never used the word 'modern'. The final official title, *De Ecclesia in Mundo Huius Temporis,* means, literally, 'The Church in the World of this Time' i.e. contemporary.

This might be dismissed as so much semantic pedantry but the confusion is revealing in that it exposes the real meaning of the word 'modern': it obviously refers to what is 'contemporary'. And this is exactly what the word was intended to mean in the Middle Ages and what probably most people now implicitly mean by it – the only problem being that 'contemporary' is a very relative term, constantly passing and in a state of flux, as what is seen to be contemporary moves on. Which is interesting because this process of constant change is not only an essential feature of what it means to be modern, but the change is driven more by technological innovation than anything else. So 'modern' has come to mean the latest bit of gadgetry or the life style that accompanies it in the contemporary world.

But this is also confusing. For the very terrorists who are supposed to be a threat to modernity have proved most adept at using

---

2. G. Tyrrell, *Medievalism.* (Longmans, 1908).

modern technology and most of those involved in the attack on the Twin Towers had technical backgrounds of higher education. They were in fact a product of modernity. But using the instruments of what is modern to attack people who live a modern lifestyle opens up an underlying contradiction as to values and motives. This contradiction with its latent instability and conflicting 'life-worlds', is, in the words of the sociologist Peter Berger, what now makes people so 'conversion prone'[3] This is all an essential part of what it means to be modern, and being able to live in proximity to difference – be it colour, belief or life-style – is perhaps the greatest challenge of modernity.

It was precisely this issue that *Gaudium et Spes* sought to address with its policy of entering into a dialogue of discernment so as to read 'the signs of the times' – a key phrase. Certainly this is an admirable way of overcoming fear of the 'other': to seek understanding. But again it comes at the price of confusion. The first casualty of dialogue is stereotypes – people are not what we thought them to be – but if a realisation that differences are not so monolithic is the beginning, the consequence is a blurring of boundaries and fusing of identities, which can be disconcerting and disorienting. This has the potential to introduce instability and mayhem into institutions like the church. So the whole process was surreptitiously strangulated (under the pontificate of John Paul II).

In this new dispensation, modernity is something deviant. Essentially, it has run off the rails and stands in radical need of correction, with the help of traditional wisdom. The point where modernity supposedly went off the rails and began to go wrong can be variously ascribed. In religious circles the point of defection is often seen as the Reformation, which initiated a future of endless fragmentation and controversy.[4] In secular academic circles and among right-wing politicians the point of defection is the Enlightenment of the eighteenth century: the 'so called European Enlightenment' in the withering put-down of John Paul II, who went on to elaborate on

---

3. P. Berger, *The Homeless Mind* (Penguin, 1974).
4. J. Mohler, *Symbolik* (Mainz, 1832), in which he argued that the Roman Catholic Church alone had remained impervious to the crippling internecine conflicts of Protestantism.

nature of modern secularism that, 'Over the years I have become more and more convinced that the ideologies of evil are profoundly rooted in the history of European philosophical thought.'[5] One can almost hear the deafening applause from American Republican neocons and evangelicals, though one may also wonder at the long history of genocidal anti-Semitism and crusading movements rooted in Christendom which seemed to have slipped his memory.[6]

But then, as Don Cupitt sagely pointed out, modernity is not an ideology at all, 'but something more like a process or a fate that has been overtaking us for centuries.'[7] Central to this process is critical thinking, something that is deeply, and uniquely, embedded in Western civilisation and derives, ironically, from its biblical roots and Christian tradition of ascetic scrutiny of one's innermost thoughts and morals. In time, the penchant for religious scrupulosity has given way to the practice of scientific methodology with its ongoing obsessiveness over the evaluation of detail and its never more than tentative conclusions. The process of secularisation which characterises modernity has risen historically and inexorably from its Christian antecedents, the bridge over which we cross to a new understanding of life simply focused on itself. In this sense Christianity is not just another religion, but the religion which leads to the end of religion: the 'religion of the "exit" from religion'.[8] Paradoxically, at its most profound level, the aetiology of modernity is to be found in Europe's Christian past.[9]

---

5. John Paul II, *Memory and Identity: Personal Reflections* (Phoenix, 2005).
6. It is no coincidence that Hitler code named his invasion of the Soviet Union 'Operation Barbarossa' after the great medieval crusading Holy Roman Emperor, Frederick I, and anticipated the destruction of Communism as the fulfilment of Germany's historic (and sacred) mission to 'civilise' the Slavic people begun by the crusades of the Teutonic Knights. Larry Siedentop argues persuasively in *Inventing the Individual: The Origins of Western Liberalism* (Allan Lane, 2014) in favour of the view that the Enlightenment was rooted in its Christian past, which was 'the ultimate source of the social revolution that has made the West what it is.' P. 353.
7. D. Cupitt, *The Meaning of The West* (SCM, 2008) p.89.
8. M. Gauchet, *The Disenchantment of the World*, quoted in C. Davis, *Religion and the Making of Society* (Cambridge, 1994), p.3.
9. Amongst the first to put forward this thesis was Karl Lowith in *Meaning in History* (Chicago, 1949), following the prophetic writing of Dietrich Bonhoeffer on the coming of 'religionless Christianity'.

In the sense of what the pope was saying – that the evils of atheistic Nazism and Communism were the inevitable outcome of the Enlightenment – this is not too different from what John Gray (professor of European Thought at the London School of Economics) is also in the habit of saying.[10] Insofar as the Enlightenment created the modern world, he writes, so 'death camps are as modern as laser surgery'; for the Nazis being modern meant racial conquest and genocide.[11] If this is being modern then, indeed, we are all better off not being modern: enter post-modernism, with its rejection of the values of progress and human perfectibility, which were the cornerstone of Enlightenment thinking.

This has now become a widely pervasive thesis. It also expresses itself in the rise of religious fundamentalism, with its rejection of rationality and unapologetic trashing of modernity in favour of a deeper, religiously rooted past. As Gray also comments, 'We live in a post-secular time.' But however good this sounds as polemic, it is – as Roy Porter noted in his ground-breaking re-appraisal of the Enlightenment[12] – 'historical baloney.' After all, the Nazis loathed the Enlightenment *philosophes* and derived their key inspiration from writers like Herder and Fichte, who were Romantic reactionaries with an equal loathing of the Enlightenment: as Herder said, 'I am not here to think, but to be, feel, live.'[13] The formulation of the 'gothic' German Romantic reaction in the early nineteenth century was to counter what was seen as the threat of 'modern' French rationalism. The Enlightenment (mainly English and French) was as

---

10. J. Gray, *Black Mass: Apocalyptic Religion and the Death of Utopia* (Penguin, 2007).
11. J. Gray, *Straw Dogs: Thoughts on Humans and Other Animals* (Granta, 2002).
12. R. Porter, *Enlightenment: Britain and the Creation of the Modern World* (Penguin, 2001).
13. Quoted, I. Berlin, *The Crooked Timber of Humanity* (John Murray, 1990), p. 40. What is often overlooked in the confrontation between religious idealism and secular ideology is that they are two sides of the same millenarian coin in which one sees the future in terms of a supernatural destiny and the other as a natural utopian dream: both are 'messianic', both demand absolute faith, both despise doubters/heretics, neither have time for individual deviation, as one of Stalin's acolytes said of his role in the great collectivisation programme in 1933 'I saw people dying … corpses in the melting snow … I saw all this … Nor did I lose my faith. I believed because I wanted to believe.' Quoted in Catherine Merridale, *Night of Stone: Death and Memory in Russia* (Granta, 2000), p. 219.

different from Romanticism (German) as chalk and cheese. To the Nazis *Aufklärung* (enlightenment) meant 'propaganda' – which is not too far removed from what it meant at the Vatican (as in *propaganda fide* – the teaching of the faith).

All this reflects the vertiginous cross currents of modernity and the perilous reefs it disguises. In fact the significance of the Enlightenment for what it means to be modern is far more disturbing than any of this. What it signifies is a mental change that constitutes one of the few great epistemic mutations in the history of human culture, such as the Ionian Enlightenment and Axial Age of the sixth century BC.[14] Its significance lay not just in new ideas or inventions or values but in the emergence of a radically different way of understanding the world which marks the 'pre-modern' from the 'modern' – regardless of time or place.

This change has sometimes been pinpointed to the change from understanding knowledge as 'correspondence' to knowledge as 'representation'.[15] In the former, Platonic and medieval, view, the world we see corresponds to a hidden 'real' but arcane world of spiritual powers and beings controlling our world, which is but a shell of resemblance, a world of excrescences and demi-urges. In contrast, in the modern world view analogy has been replaced by verifiable knowledge, empirically based, which can be tested through a measured methodology.[16] In short, a world which is simply itself and nothing more.

The consequences of this change for our understanding of the world have been profound. It has caused previous pivotal assumptions to be abandoned: for example, that there is a beginning to things, that there is a *uni*-verse, that there is a stable order with an underlying intelligent design, that there is a purpose or destiny to things. All this has gone, to leave an arbitrary cosmos based on

---

14. The phrase 'Axial Age' was coined by philosopher Karl Jaspers for the period 800–200 BC. Cf. K. Armstrong, *The Great Transformation: The World in the Time of Buddha, Socrates, Confucius and Jeremiah.* (Atlantic, 2007). The phrase 'Ionian Enlightenment' belongs to A. N. Whitehead, *Adventures of Ideas* (Free Press, 1933) and is more focused on the seminal advances in Greek thought around the sixth century BC. Both challenged 'traditional' religions.
15. J. Merquior, *Foucault* (Fontana, 1991), particularly p. 45.
16. Cf. C. Davis, *Religion and the Making of Society* (Cambridge, 1994), p. 25.

chance and necessity, where random mutations produce new beginnings.[17] In this scenario the universe is an accident and life a 'mistake'. This understanding is at the heart of what now passes for modernity, which 'refuses submission to anything that attempts to impose itself upon human consciousness from without.'[18] No wonder people cling to the consolation of older, 'pre-modern' myths.

Not that there is anything inevitable about being modern. Though there is a general assumption that we are all now more or less modern and will become more so, John Gray argues that nothing could be further from the truth.[19] The roll call of twentieth century dictatorships, from Stalin to Pol, is one of unprecedented and in parts incomprehensible savagery, even barbarism, legitimated by modern utopian beliefs. So much for the central myth of modernity, 'progress'. On the basis of a simple majority count the US, once a paragon of modernity, with its current vocal creationist lobby, neocon evangelicals and democratic elitism, is less 'modern' now than it was in the eighteenth century.[20] It is now no more 'modern' than say Iran. So, it may well be that the Enlightenment enterprise of modernity, with its hallmarks of reason and science, is repudiated and abandoned. Modernity could re-introduce new forms of Stone Age tribalism – in the Khmer Rouge it already has.

In what has been called 'the pathology of modernity' the process of rationalisation or the gradual rise of reason in history – a grand Hegelian theme – has not led to greater freedom but to what the

---

17. J. Monod (1971), *Chance and Necessity* (Penguin, 1997).
18. Davis, *ibid.* p. 23.
19. J. Gray, *Al Qaeda and What it Means to be Modern* (Faber & Faber, 2003).
20. Typically, influential Republican Senator, Jim Inhofe, happily dismisses 'all this "Soviet-style" liberal scientific stuff' (it all gets a bit mixed up!) about climate change: 'My point is, God's still up there' so 'the arrogance of people to think that we human beings would be able to change what He (God) is doing in climate is to me outrageous.' With views like these and a book entitled *The Greatest Hoax: How the Global Warming Conspiracy Threatens Your Future,* he has been appointed chair of the Senate Environment and Public Works Committee, which determines future US policy. (Report, *The Independent,* 11 Nov. 2014) On a more general level the US-based evangelical group, the World Congress of Families, which opposes gay rights, thinks, 'Civilisation is on the verge of destruction, and only Russia can become a centre of consolidation of all the healthy forces and resistance to the sodomisation of the world.' Now listen for Benjamin Franklin spinning in his grave!

sociologist Max Weber, called the 'iron cage' of bureaucratic rationality, from which there is no escape. This is the rationality of the modern state with its techniques and calculation, organisation and administration controlling all our lives. One aspect of this was the emergence, in the nineteenth century, of the grand post-Hegelian ideological systems bearing the suffix 'ism'. Another was the effect of imperial outreach, with its desire for order and regulation, on the old religious traditions of the world so as to create new synthetic amalgams: Hindu-ism, Buddh-ism, Tao-ism, Shinto-ism, etc.[21] Leading finally, of course, to the modern curse of the caged mind that is fundamental-ism.

The Twin Towers in New York were symbols of modernity; their destruction also a consequence of modernity. Demonstrably modern in architecture, brash and over-bearing, built for the pursuit of self-interest and the accumulation of capital: a massive two fingers to anyone who thought otherwise. Their presence and the agenda of global capitalism could not but provoke antipathy from other, adverse 'isms' – the equal and opposite reaction, just as Hegel predicted.[22] Some of these might seem to be in the form of a traditional backlash but, as Gregory Baum wrote of Catholicism in its condemnation of modernism, 'Whenever a religion vehemently rejects a modern society, it integrates certain elements of modernity into the new formed orthodoxy.'[23] They too are modern.

Modernity was never lacking in ambition; it was always about taking over the Earth. Its mission, from the time of Sir Francis Bacon on, has been to wrest nature's secrets from her; it was meant to abolish mystery with the light of reason. But in doing so it has threatened to destroy the Earth, only to reveal yet greater mysteries, and with them the certainty that we will never know them. For our knowledge is strictly proportionate to the power of our senses and, though we have been clever enough to extend their scope through technical

21. C. Bayly, *The Birth of the Modern World 1780–1914* (Blackwell, 2004), ch.9: 'Empires of Religion'.
22. T. Ali, *The Clash of Fundamentalisms: Crusades, Jihads and Modernity* (Verso, 2002), also Z. Sardar & M Davies, *Why do People Hate America?* (Icon, 2003).
23. G. Baum in the Introduction to E. Leonard, *George Tyrrell and the Catholic Tradition* (Darton, Longman and Todd, 1982).

gadgetry, still only a small fraction of one possible universe has been revealed. According to the Astronomer Royal, Martin Rees, the rest will always remain beyond our grasp.[24] The 'Dream of Reason' that launched modernity is destined to remain for ever a dream.

Everything is now so tentative and relative. Matter is energy and energy is evanescent, here today gone tomorrow, so 'contemporary', so 'modern'. In becoming aware of its limits, ambiguities and contradictions, we are already in the realms of post-modern irony, with its endless 'scare' marks. Amidst rising global tensions fomented in part by the growing rejection of secular critical thinking in favour of religious radicalism, we now live in the penumbra of the Enlightenment. In this sense perhaps modernity has indeed already 'ended'.

24.M. Rees, *The Final Century: Will the Human Race Survive the Twenty-First Century?* (Heinemann, 2008).

CHAPTER 8

Moving On

How change has come to characterise modernity

'To live is to change'. These memorable words of Cardinal Newman have come to epitomise the basic reality of our age. Transience is everything. Substantial works have analysed how cultural and scientific change takes place; a whole industry has grown up around how to manage change. But while leaders look forward to new horizons the groundswell of dissent prefers to look back to the familiar. This resistance to change and preference for tradition is associated with another feature of modernity: the growth of fundamentalism, a word perceptively restructured as 'founder-mentality'. The desire is to go back to reassuring authoritative figures of the past for guidance in the modern age: Moses, Jesus, Mohamed, Nanak ... Look no further, their teachings were enough![1]

The irony here is that such figures were invariably prime examples of agents of change in their own times.[2] An early criticism of Christianity (by the pagan philosopher Celsus) was of its novelty. He complained that it had none of the attributes of a proper religion – temples, altars, sacrifices, priesthood, etc.[3] Adaption to new social and political circumstances soon changed that, as the historian Peter Brown noted: 'a glance at the art and secular culture of the later (Roman) empire makes one fact abundantly clear; when the 'governing elite' of this officially Christian empire presented themselves to themselves and to the world at large ... the 'set of symbolic forms'

---

1. L. Geering. *Reimagining God* (Polebridge, 2014), particularly ch.10: 'Idolatry in the Church', where he coins the word 'bibliolatry' for the obsessive adherence to the literal meaning of texts, which becomes a form of idolatry and substitute for thought.
2. K. Armstrong. *The Great Transformation: The World in the Time of Buddha, Socrates, Confucius and Jeremiah* (Atlantic, 2004).
3. E. Dodds. *Christians and Pagans in an Age of Anxiety: Aspects of Religious Experience from Marcus Aurelius to Constantine* (Cambridge, 1965).

by which they expressed this fact owed little or nothing to Christianity.'[4] By the fifth century Christianity had changed out of all recognition.

One doesn't have to be a paid-up Marxist to concede that economics promotes social change from which arise changes of understanding – Marxism was itself a product of such change. Similarly, the discovery of new and anomalous facts produces new theories.[5] As the economist J. M. Keynes once quipped, 'When the facts change I change my mind, what do you do, sir?' Or, in the imagery of religious writing, a once discarded stone can become the cornerstone of a new edifice of belief. This metaphor exemplifies the true 'founder-mentality', of looking into the depths of things and being prepared to rethink.

But opening up to change can be portrayed as betrayal. Ever since Zarathustra – perhaps the first truly innovative religious thinker – was stabbed in the back by a member of the traditional hierarchy (*karapan*), things have never been easy for the reformer.[6] The standard suspicion of the convert is one of untrustworthiness: why trust someone who got it wrong before, and having changed once might change again. Both Newman and St Paul were subject to such suspicion. Yet, if anything, it disguises a deeper illusion: that to have changed once is sufficient. One must continue to move on, and had St Paul owned up to the fact that his eschatology (that there would be a Second Coming of Christ in his lifetime) was wrong, his ethical precepts would have been more realistic. Had Newman perceived that his key theory of the development of Christian doctrine failed to grasp the real meaning of evolution (random mutation or change), his theology would have been even more radical. In a nutshell, the failure of both these historical colossi was that in having changed, they failed to change further.

Perhaps the role model that religious institutions most lack is of the founder who changes *again*; of the founder who lives on the

---

4. P. Brown. *Authority and the Sacred: Aspects of the Christianisation of the Roman World* (Cambridge University Press, 1995), p. 11.
5. D. Boorstin. *The Discoverers: A History of Man's Search to Know his World and Himself* (Phoenix, 1983).
6. P. Kriwaczek. *In Search of Zarathustra: The First Prophet and the Ideas that Changed the World* (Weidenfeld & Nicolson, 2002).

move, for whom there are no final solutions. The inspirational pope, John XXIII became such a person. His famous death-bed admonition to be bold, look far into the future and prepare for further change was exemplary.[7] It is a vision the current Pope Francis is trying to reclaim. St. Augustine – a man who had undergone much change – gave some inkling of the model for such change in his exhortation, 'Linger not by the way, always press on, always advance.'

Such a view is not dissimilar to the idea of the Church as a 'pilgrim people', espoused by the Vatican Council II. But even this has subsequently been deemed suspect by traditionalists, who would argue that the implication of a Church *in via* is that there is some lack or deficiency yet to be found, which conflicts with the view of the Church as an already perfected institution. But even the idea of 'pilgrimage' is an insufficient model of the change which modernity presses upon us. For the change of which we are speaking has neither goal nor road; rather it is the art of the surfer, breasting the resurgent waves of change – a transience that leaves no trace.

This is an altogether more alarming notion – a dizziness, hovering on the brink of chaos. The fundamental feature of primeval chaos is of a chthonic, surging darkness, against which the light of religious revelation has always defined its ordered cosmologies. Today we understand things differently. Chaos is now viewed positively as the essential underlying feature of complex systems. The science of complexity – of which Chaos Theory is a part – shows how very small random changes lead to new systems, totally disproportionate to their origins.[8] Life itself only becomes possible within this state of dynamic equilibrium. Everything is marvellously balanced on the edge of chaos but constantly reordering and renewing itself, such as the ecological systems of the Earth.

This is how we have now come to understand reality. As theoretical physicist John Barrow writes, 'The science of how complex systems organise themselves is currently one of the great frontiers of

---

7. P. Hebblethwaite. *Pope John XXII: Pope of the Council* (Geoffrey Chapman, 1984), p. 499: 'Those who have lived as long as I have... know that the moment has come to discern the signs of the times, to seize the opportunity and to look far ahead.'

8. M. Buchanan. *Ubiquity: the Science of History or why the World is Simpler than we Think* (Phoenix, 2000).

scientific research.'[9] It has implications for everything about us: economics, ecology, weather, even the workings of the human mind. Life has taken on the aspect of an emergent, self-organising drama that embraces the whole universe.[10] Thanks to the work of modern cosmologists we can now see that the elements which make life possible are part of the universe in its current phase of expansion.

But if life itself has such a vast and arbitrary context, the theological pre-eminence of humanity – 'man' – in the universe begins to look arbitrary. Soteriology (theories of redemption) centred on ourselves and our own rather insignificant planet now look rather parochial. Yet the great religious and ethical systems as we now know them have all assumed, rather innocuously, the centrality of humanity in their grand theandric dramas, just as pre-Copernican man assumed the centrality of the Earth in the cosmic order. In this scheme of things nature provided the peripheral backdrop, or (as in the Franciscan theology of St. Bonaventure) the amphitheatre, of a divine drama.

The idea of a created cosmic order has long been closely tied to the concept of a stable, comprehensible and unique universe. When this concept first arose amongst the Ionian thinkers of ancient Greece, it was seen as seditious, detracting from the role of the gods. Monistic thinking – as with its surrogate, monotheism – gained ascendancy at first only as a superior type of *gnosis*, held by elites in the face of popular incomprehension and hostility. It could be life-threatening for those who voiced such views in the face of well-established deities, as both Greek philosophers and Jewish prophets found to their cost. But now, far from being a superior idea, it looks distinctly dated. As Bishop John Robinson remarked in 1963, 'Our image of God as a personal being must go.' As monotheism now evolves into a simpler *monism,* beliefs in such figures as the great Jehovah or Allah are to be seen as mere staging posts on a wider exploration.[11]

---

9. J. Barrow, *Theories of Everything: The Quest for Ultimate Explanations* (Vintage, 1991).
10. S. Kauffman, *At Home in the Universe: The Search for the Laws of Complexity* (Penguin, 1995).
11. L. Geering, *ibid.* ch.8: 'How Humans Made God'.

The challenge now facing us is to move on from our previous ideological camps and comfort zones to give priority to life, the matrix of everything that is. This entails a new exodus into the unknown. Man, as the patriarchal monotheist with 'super'-natural ambitions lording it over creation, must change. The theologian and 'geologian', Thomas Berry was clear that, 'The present disruption of all the basic life systems of Earth has come about within a culture that emerged from a biblical-Christian matrix.' It emerged within our Western Christian-derived civilisation, whose view of 'stewardship' of nature 'does not recognise that nature has prior stewardship over us.'[12] James Lovelock was even more scathing: 'The idea that humans are yet intelligent enough to serve as stewards of the Earth is amongst the most hubristic ever.'[13]

As a result we are now confronted with a remarkable sense of apocalypse of our own making; a sense that our survival is in our own hands and that we must change. In this context the abasement or self-emptying humanity must undergo for survival is a remarkable simulacrum of the theological drama of redemption described by St. Paul in his letter to the Philippians.[14] Redemption entailed the humbling of the redeemer, *kenosis*/self-emptying; our survival entails an end to human hubris and a humbling of our ambitions. We, who have shaped imaginative theandric dramas must now be even more imaginative and reshape our own. For this, radical changes in thinking and acting are required.

Amongst others, the philosopher George Santayana, presciently grappled with this challenge. Though he recognised there was something in man that led him constantly to rebel against naturalism in favour of some kind of eternal ideal, he also recognised that hankering after the 'denatured' forms of old beliefs was to be like Don Quixote tinkering with obsolete armour. For him 'the word *nature* is poetical enough' (*Scepticism and Animal Faith*).[15] Though in some way nostalgic for the old certainties of belief he, perhaps reluctantly, accepted that modern science revealed that, outside the human sphere,

12. T. Berry in *The Christian Future and the Fate of the Earth* (Orbis, 2009) pp. 35-36.
13. J. Lovelock, *The Revenge of Gaia* (Allen Lane, 2006).
14. Philippians 2: 6-11.
15. Quoted in W. Durant, *The Story of Philosophy* (Pocket Library, 1954), ch.11.

all is chaotic and beyond our control: 'no doubt the spirit and energy of the world is what is acting in us, as the sea that rises in every little wave ... Our privilege is to have perceived it as it moved.' *(Life of Reason).*[16] Now we must move on.

From a necessary kenotic humbling follows a whole new way of living, centred not on rights but respect, of a willingness to curtail rights (of reproduction, consumption and comfort) out of respect for the natural order that our recklessness has brought to the point of destruction. The supernatural narrative of monotheism is now replaced by the natural narrative of *monozoism,* one life. Whatever religious beliefs humanity may choose to retain in the future will no doubt continue to have social and personal value as cultural attributes derived from past traditions. But the test of their acceptability will be their compatibility with the survival of the great web of life, of which we are but a part. Life embraces all that *is* – changing, evolving, evanescent. To complete the words of Cardinal Newman, 'To have lived long is to have changed much.'

---

16. Durant, *ibid.*

CHAPTER 9

In Need of a Story

How consciousness explains the world

We all enjoy a good story. Perhaps, one could go further and say, we all need a good story. At one point in her BBC radio series on *Belief,* Joan Bakewell asked the award winning story teller Philip Pullman if it is the nature of consciousness to explain itself in stories.[1] With this he agreed: 'This hunger for working out how things came about (the story), is tremendously deep' – it's almost an insatiable need, and once we've heard how one thing came about, we then want to know about the next thing. A story is a fundamental way in which we come to an understanding of our world – a 'little speck of light in the middle of a great, vast encircling darkness; which is everything I don't know'. It's the darkness, the unknown, the mystery which gives the *frisson* of excitement and engrossment.

And it's not just about understanding 'what's out there'. It's also about explaining – or at least, coming to terms with – ourselves. The cognitive theorist Daniel Dennett has even gone so far as to claim that we are our own story, that the self is nothing more or less than the 'centre of narrative gravity' within the brain. Neatly reversing what we might first expect – in a true story teller's *coup de foudre* – he even claims (in *Consciousness Explained*) that for the most part our tales are spun not by us, but us by them: 'Our human consciousness, and our narrative selfhood, is their product, not their source.' This is the inner darkness of the self into which neurology has shone its increasingly revealing light.

It could be argued – as Dennett does – that all this is the result of the enormous brain power of humans, way beyond the basic biological needs for survival. Instead of just focusing on the job in hand, our imaginings are all over the place. Indeed, the first clear sign of

---

1. Now published as: Joan Bakewell, *Belief* (Duckworth, 2005), p. 172.

homo sapiens is the appearance of symbolic graffiti on cave walls.[2] It's as if we have a compulsion to express an inner world, centred somewhere in our heads, reaching out to make contact with an outer world, desperately trying to make sense of things, linking up the information coming to us from the external world. It's the story, above all else, which enables us to put all the pieces together: it provides not only the map of the world but our place in it, and our place then provides our identity.

From the earliest shamans – mediating between worlds and declaiming their story – the provision of meta-narratives has traditionally been the domain of religion, with its over-arching cosmic myths and rituals of initiation. These are the stories of perennial appeal that have underpinned our cultural understanding: one popular re-rendering of the Bible was aptly entitled *The Greatest Story Ever Told*. But we have increasingly come to see these stories for what they are, stories – the creations of human consciousness. As theoretical physicist John Barrow cryptically points out, myths do not arise from data or as solutions to practical problems 'They emerge as antidotes for mankind's psychological suspicion of smallness and insignificance in the face of things he cannot understand.'[3]

In modern times the shaman's wand has been replaced not only by the scientist's probe but by the novelist's pen as the delineator of the order of things. As writer and academic David Lodge summarises in his study of how the novel has served as a vehicle of consciousness, *Consciousness and the Novel*, 'Increasingly, as we move into the modern period, the emphasis falls on the construction of the real within the individual's consciousness, the difficulty of communication between these separate mental worlds, the distorting effects of the unconscious on consciousness and the limits of human understanding.'[4] This is the domain of the modern story teller, and there are no bounds to his artifice. No doubt the overwhelming appeal of Tolkien lies in his ability not only to tell stories but, through

---

2. Cf. David Lewis-Williams, *The Mind in the Cave: Consciousness and the Origins of Art* (Thames & Hudson, 2004).
3. John Barrow, *Theories of Everything* (Vintage, 1991), p. 5.
4. David Lodge, *Consciousness and the Novel* (Penguin, 2002), p. 49.

them, to conjure up whole worlds with their own orders of beings and languages.

But the story is far more than an individual need, it is a collective one and in modern times this has also undergone a radical transformation. In a fascinating study of revolutionary Europe in the century between 1776 and 1871, Adam Zamoyski charts how romantics and patriots created new cultural understanding which transformed the nature of our collective stories. The thesis of his book, *Holy Madness,* is that as a result of the waning of religion as a universal value system, post-Enlightenment men and women turned to nationalism to fill the void left by God; revolutionaries hoped to construct a paradise on Earth rather than wait for one in heaven. Indeed, revolution was the new theology: 'The theology may have been shaky, but the new religion did have a god. That god was the sovereign nation, whose service was the highest calling.'[5]

To satisfy this new outlook there was a growing desire for stories of origin. Amongst the first and most influential provider was the Scotsman James Macpherson who, in the 1750s, produced translations of, supposedly, ancient Gaelic poetry he claimed to have discovered whilst travelling around the highlands and islands of Scotland. Published under the name of a putative ancient bard, *The Works of Ossian* were an instant success across Europe. Purporting to reveal an ancient wisdom and a nobler way of life, now occluded by civilisation, Macpherson addressed a deep yearning for a different sort of world – a world of drama and excitement, as he wrote, 'An unsettled state, and those convulsions which attend it, is the proper field for an exalted character.' As well as a good story, what he and other Romantics – for this is what they were, 'romancers' – were really searching for, if not inventing, was, as Zamoyski says, 'a spiritual *patrie,* a sort of church, to which to belong.' It is a vein still being vigorously quarried by New Age aficionados.

Regardless of the fact that, as Dr Johnson surmised, the works were forgeries – bearing as much resemblance to any real historical past as does Tolkien's Middle Earth – they inspired similar forages into a mythical past across Europe. This was particularly the case in

5. Adam Zamoyski, *Holy Madness; Romantics, Patriots and Revolutionaries:* 1776–1871 (Weidenfeld & Nicholson, 1999).

Germany, where the influential poet and philologist Johann Herder conjectured humanity to be divided into groups, each belonging to an idealised original people, or *Volk*, distinguished by language, experience, homeland and destiny. The evidence of this ancient *Volk* was deemed to be hidden in the collective consciousness of remote communities. In a neat reversal of the earlier phase of Europe's Christianisation, what was called for was not missionaries but emissaries, sent not to proclaim but reclaim. So began a movement, exemplified by the brothers Grimm, to reveal the *epos* and linguistic roots of the *Volk*.

What was really happening across Europe was the formation and expression of a new mentality or *Zeitgeist*. Far from being fairy tales for children, this was a serious and ominous business: nothing less than the creation of national self-consciousness. Macpherson imagined a past characterised by the 'manly pursuits from which barbarity takes its name', which created 'a strength of mind unknown in polished times'. Rousseau provided the political agenda of 'the noble savage'. This, when combined with social discontent and the view of history provided by Herder and Hegel, as a process in which nations continuously struggle to achieve self-fulfilment, produced an incendiary cocktail that would ultimately plunge Europe into a state of unimaginable barbarism and world war. Fairy tales had become nightmares.

In our own time we have come to see how disastrously mistaken this whole understanding has been. So much so that it has left us with a guilty reticence to voice the previous national stories of identity. Thus the vacuum has been recreated which such stories were once intended to fill. What remains is a sense of confusion, so noticeable in the recent referenda on the proposed European Constitution, of wanting a national identity but uncertain how to express it. This inchoate desire is really the need, once more, for a story which can provide some over-arching sense of value and a reference point for understanding. Our need is for a story more in keeping with the reality of the world; one which is not just a region of the mind, dreamed up by the poetic imagination, fuelled by turbulent emotions and fetid nostalgia.

My contention is that the basis for such a story already lies before us in the great evolutionary saga which we now understand to have shaped all that is. It is a saga awesome to behold, full of mystery and wonder, splendid in its manifestations yet dark beyond our deepest imaginings.[6] It is a saga which not only brings all people together but all creatures into an intimate family and close proximity. Yet it is disturbingly different in that it rejects all sense of preordination or destiny; it is a story rooted in the chance and necessity of the present moment, without recourse to any supernatural agents. It is a story not of fate but of entanglement – to use the latest cosmological theory – of everything with everything else; a never-ending drama, in which we are not the first nor last and certainly not the most important players.

If this seems a very different sort of story from what we are used to, perhaps it is not so very different from the world of those stories uncovered by the brothers Grimm. There we also find stories full of inexplicable darkness and unexpected light, where nothing is quite as it seems and the boundaries between people, animals and things are remarkably porous – frogs become princes, birds become maidens, trees speak. Here also, chance and necessity rule, sometimes with cruel, sometimes with happy consequences. It is the animistic world, familiar to ancient shamans. But now there is a difference, and it lies at the level of intelligibility: we can now discern the basis of the coherence of things in their simplicity and complexity. Whereas Shakespeare could vaguely affirm: 'There is a destiny that shapes our ends, rough hew them as we will', and Rilke that destiny is but 'the sense-laden impressions of childhood', we can understand it as the gene laden ancestry that binds one to all.

Perhaps this story comes inevitably at the end of all other stories, but in a way that gathers the other stories together in a conscious embrace.[7] It is a pattern exemplified in one of the stories of the Hasidim narrated by Martin Buber. There was once a holy old man who lived in the forest and when people were in any sort of trouble, they would journey into the forest and he would give them God's blessing; they would return happy with their troubles lifted. Then the

---

6. See, for example, Brian Swimme & Thomas Berry, *The Universe Story* (Arkana, 1992).
7. Cf. Edward O. Wilson, *Consilience: The Unity of Knowledge* (Abacus, 1998) and Fritjof Capra, *The Hidden Connections* (Flamingo, 2002) for the ultimate story of human understanding.

holy man died, but still people would journey into the forest and pray in the place where he lived; they would return happy with their troubles lifted. In time memories faded but the tradition lived on that if you had troubles you should journey into the forest; this people did and returned happy with their troubles lifted.[8] In the end we just tell the story; we are happy and our troubles lift, as the story telling works its magic.

Here, in nutshell – or in a story – we have a history of what we have come to know as disenchantment or secularisation. The world has changed, or rather the world has stayed the same and our understanding of it has changed. But the need for a story lives on. So let us tell stories and be happy in the knowledge that all our imaginings are but stories.

---

8. Martin Buber, *Tales of the Hasidim* (Schocken, 1947).

CHAPTER 10

Patterns in the Mind

Moving beyond ideology

Before sitting down to write this chapter I arrange my thoughts. Mulling over an idea that presents itself I turn it around like a prism and see how it reflects the light of reality. Then, whilst walking the dog, I ponder further what bits of evidence may support or contradict it, what facts may enhance it, and how a pattern may be detected before launching forward to literary construction.

Nothing original in that. The novelist George Eliot put the matter altogether more graphically in *Middlemarch,* when she presented a little 'parable' regarding the habit people have of seeing patterns in events that concern them. Consider the surface of polished steel rubbed by the housemaid that, 'will be minutely and multitudinously scratched in all directions; but place now against it a lighted candle as a centre of illumination, and lo! the scratches will all seem to arrange themselves in a fine series of concentric circles round that little sun.'[1] Looked at impartially the scratches are going everywhere, it is only the light of consciousness – our 'egoism' – that gives 'the faltering illusion of concentric arrangement.'

When not writing novels, Eliot was well known as a translator of contemporary German theo-philosophical writers. Though Hegel was not one of these, she would have been only too well aware of the shadow cast by this seminal thinker of the nineteenth century. Prompted by the events of his time, the 'lighted candle' of Hegel's gargantuan consciousness spanned a vast historical spectrum, and lo! 'the flattering illusion' of a patterned process appeared. For better or worse, Hegel introduced the Western mind to the notion of historical development and change as one over-arching spiritual process. It has beguiled people ever since and as Paul Tillich wrote, 'Hegel was the

---

1. George Eliot, *Middlemarch* (OUP, 1996), ch. 27: p. 248.

centre and turning point of a world-historical movement which has directly or indirectly influenced our whole century.'[2]

It is from the time of Hegel – the end of the eighteenth century – that the grand ideological construct (the 'ism') first appeared in the English language. It has been multiplying ever since: Hegelianism mutating into Marxism – its even more influential offspring – and so on down to Maoism and our own conflicted times. Nor was it just a matter of intellectual conjecture. Having detected the pattern in the historical 'scratchings' of humanity, the great helmsmen of history surfing the currents of political change went one better: they began to rearrange history according to their conjecture. Untold millions of lives were 'rearranged' so as to confirm the flattering illusions of these great 'egoists'. The 'pattern' of history demanded nothing less.

Nothing original in any of this either. So has it always been. There is in fact a sterile controversy that periodically rears its head as to which were the more destructive of humanity: the secular ideologies of modern times or the religious beliefs of the more distant past. What this controversy obscures is that both were different sides of the same coin: the great visionaries and leaders of mankind were all partial to the 'illusion of (the) concentric arrangement' of humanity into patterns – some even claiming this to be under the illumination of revelation or, as George Washington thought, 'a special providence.'

So it continues.[3] The world is fragmented into vast ideological camps, defined by their 'isms', which increasingly rage at each other in fury. In the aftermath of the Cold War it became apparent that no Soviet general had ever met a Western counterpart (or vice versa): they were speaking to a virtual creation entirely of their own imagining, as they addressed their adversaries across the air waves. There was a brief time when it was hoped we would learn from such experience and that globalisation would bring humanity together in one grand 'concentric arrangement'. But it was not to be.

---

2. P. Tillich, *Shaking the Foundations* (Penguin, 1949).
3. Cf. C. Longley, *Chosen People: The Big Idea that shaped Britain and America* (2003). Also, John Gray, *Black Mass: Apocalyptic Religion and the Death of Utopia* (Penguin, 2007).

Now neo-cons and fundamentalists have both detected further patterns. For political neo-cons the 'global democratic revolution' has become a parody of the old Soviet plan of historical inevitability (with capitalism now replacing Leninism). Contemporary theo-philosophers like Alister McGrath have detected another pattern, in which secular society is seen as no more than a historical blip when we pretended religion was irrelevant.[4] So a religious revivalist like Jerry Jenkins (co-author of *Left Behind,* the best selling evangelical work in the USA) can claim, 'Now there are so many of us, they have to listen to us and do things our way.' Which is also what a billion Muslims are also now saying.

Others are not so sure. Richard Rorty – *bête noire* of neo-cons and traditionalists – is certainly on the side of the 'scratchings'. An un-flinching nominalist, he is committed to the view that our generalised patterns of the world are no more than the products of our own de-scriptions: 'Nominalists see language as just human beings using marks and noises to get what they want' (*Essays on Heidegger*). Fellow American philosopher, Daniel Dennett, argues that the readiness of humans to favour grand ideological and religious patterns is an unin-tentional consequence of the way our minds are constituted – a capacity that has evolved so as to enable us to detect patterns in the behaviour of others and thus anticipate them – a crucial survival asset.[5]

All of which would seem to confirm Hegel's great intuition – as revealed in his *Philosophy of History* – that 'thoughtful consideration' reveals 'a progress of the consciousness'. In this master-pattern everything finds its place, even conflicts – such as that between the ideologies of faith and unbelief, theism and atheism (those 'isms' again). So is there any way beyond the dialectic of the endlessly form-ing patterns of the mind and their constantly grinding tectonic plates?

In fact, I would suggest there is, and it becomes clear from a re-turn to the roots of Hegel's thinking in Greek thought. It was whilst reading Plato's *Dialogues* that Hegel seemed to have conceived the

---

4. A. McGrath, *The Twilight of Atheism: The Rise and Fall of Disbelief in the Modern World* (Doubleday, 2004).
5. D. Dennett, *Breaking the Spell: Religion as a Natural Phenomenon* (Penguin, 2007).

idea of history as a dialectical pattern. This was based on his understanding of the Socratic method of bringing conflicting ideas together leading to a new state of consciousness.[6] But Socrates – archdebunker of the opinionated – did not pretend this to be the basis of some grand historical process, such as Hegel extrapolated from it, but the very opposite.

For Socrates the dialogue was an existential encounter, in which personal communication does not so much give rise to a world of abstraction (a synthesis drawn from a preceding antithesis), but rather allows each to discover a new understanding of their own world. In our times the existential philosopher, Martin Buber, has reiterated a Socratic view of 'life as a meeting' as a way to deeper relationships and new understandings.[7] Genuine encounters always realise new potentialities.

Here the meaning of newness is crucial. Understanding novelty – so often seen as a threat by traditionalists – has also been a challenge to biologists seeking to understand how new species and features evolve. Interestingly, the latest thinking about natural processes throws light on our numinal associations. For example, systems biologists Marc Kirscher and John Gerhart state that novelty arises, 'by the use of conserved processes in new combinations, at different times, and in different places and amounts, rather than by the invention of new processes.'[8] Novelty, then, is not the appearance of something hitherto non-existent but rather the realisation of unexamined or unexpected implications in one's own patterned world.

As with the natural world, so with the cultural world. We can begin to see those personal 'scratchings' on the grand historical surface in a different way. Not as the fatalistic record of the prisoner on his cell wall, resigned to his historical destiny, but as the expression of a creative operative shaping his own destiny in conjunction with others. The 'scratchings' – like the 'conserved processes' of hitherto hidden capacities that give each their personality – become their own revelation, not of some grand pattern but of ourselves.

---

6. P. Singer, *Hegel: A Very Short Introduction* (Oxford, 1983).
7. A. Hodes, *Encounter with Martin Buber* (Allen Lane, 1972).
8. M. Kirschner & J. Gerhart, *The Plausibility of Life* (Yale, 2005).

On a cultural and social level what is also new is the consequent mutuality of two previously differing worlds, which are now characterised by a *shared* enrichment. In this we begin to see beyond the ideological world of grand designs, of clashing civilisations and endless conflict. In the end we just let 'the scratchings' speak for themselves. Just think if those Soviet generals had actually bothered to meet their Western counterparts!

Instead of the patterns we begin to appreciate the particularities, even peculiarities in ourselves and others. We can then begin to generate new shared understandings. This kind of mutuality allows each a breathing space and allows us to understand ourselves better. In the end we can just dispense with the patterns and 'isms' altogether. Now, where did I put that dog's lead?

CHAPTER 11

Moral Vacuums and How to Fill Them

Morality in a post-religious world

Whatever else one may, or may not, think about the philosopher Friedrich Nietzsche, one cannot deny that he had a gift for finding an apt turn of phrase. One that springs to mind is 'transvaluing all values' – that traditional values are no longer of help to modern man, who stands, bewildered, on the verge of a changed world: or 'transfigured night' (another apt phrase). The quest for a new value system was a central preoccupation of Nietzsche, who saw a kindred spirit in Zarathustra, that enigmatic primordial prophet of religious consciousness and cosmic morality, who stood at the very dawn of civilisation. If Nietzsche glimpsed the end of the whole cycle of civilisation – the Twilight of the Idols – he had a sufficient sense of irony to advise any new prophets to think of prospective disciples in terms of zeros: religious movements have had their day. Instead, he was content that each should be 'the artist of his own life', confecting a 'self-mastery morality' (*Herrenmoral*). With the bar of personal responsibility set so high, it is little wonder that most baulked at the challenge, or chose to deliberately misunderstand him, as they joined the Gadarene rush into the cataclysm that was the Great War (even with his books packed in their knapsacks).

These thoughts were prompted by the call of David Cameron to the nation to 'actively stand up and defend' the 'values and moral code' of the Bible. Speaking at a commemoration of the 400th anniversary of the publication of the King James Bible, he pointed out that, 'We are a Christian country and we should not be afraid to say so.' After all, it was the values and morals of the Bible that helped to make Britain what it is today. Beset, as we are, by a tsunami of problems that threaten to overwhelm us – problems largely of our own making – it is not surprising that a call should be made to look back from these twilight hours of national conviction to more halcyon times. But is it helpful, or simply a siren call that draws us further onto the fatal reefs of self-destruction?

Nietzsche, for one, would have been in no doubt as to the answer: he derided the 'English flatheads' (in *Twilight of the Idols*), who cannot quite grasp that the underlying convictions of modern man have shifted. As it was, 'Christianity is a system, a *whole* view of things thought out together' which is predicated on a belief in God, who alone knows what is good and evil, and presupposes that 'man does not know, *cannot* know, what is good for him.' It is this that now makes traditional morality (and identity) problematic. Instead, David Cameron reveals himself as standing in that long English tradition of pragmatism, boldly standing up for moral precepts that have been inherited without quite being able to recognise that the foundations have crumbled. If, for whatever reason, 'We don't do God', as Tony Blair's spin doctor Alistair Campbell once declared, it is difficult to argue for the traditional values that go with this belief – including the sense of divine election or 'chosenness', that has been such an integral part of national identity since Bede wrote his *History of the English Church and Nation.* Unless, of course, as Nietzsche mocked, 'the English actually believe that they know "intuitively" what is good and evil.'

So this is the place we have come to: we are not too happy where we are, and we may not be too sure about how we got into the mess we are in, but one thing we are even more fearful about is what lies before us. This is how moral vacuums open up, and not for the first time. Nor is David Cameron alone in confronting such a situation or in seeking solutions from the past. In Russia, as Vladimir Putin has sought to rein in the anarchy that followed the collapse of communism, old-fashioned nationalism and Russian Orthodoxy have their appeal and uses. In China, where the official ideology of communism survives, but has been hopelessly compromised by consumer capitalism and corruption, the authorities are once again increasingly keen to promote traditional Confucian values of respectful harmony – also a useful counter-block to human rights. In the Middle East, as societies seek to free themselves from sclerotic, compromised autocrats, the appeal is to traditional Muslim values, based on uncompromising Koranic teachings. But it is, no doubt, in the USA that Mr Cameron's call would find closest resonance, with the Republicans demanding a return to the clearly founded biblical values of the past in the fight against a demonised liberalism.

In all these cases the moral vacuum that has opened up takes its shape from a particular historic experience that precedes it, but which also suggests its own resolution – from the past. And therein lies the danger: it was the pathways from the past that brought us to the very impasse whose resolution now clearly escapes us. Take Russia. When the Nazis were at the gates of Moscow, Stalin retreated to his dacha in depression, saying to members of the Politburo gathered there, 'Lenin gave us the plan and we have screwed it up.' Of course what he should have said is not 'we' but 'he' screwed it up – through paranoia and relentless brutality. In the end it was these things, together with economic incompetence, which brought the whole system crashing down, just as it had the Czarist regime before it. When the Marquis de Custine toured Russia in 1839, he noted an 'absolute monarchy moderated by murder'. This vicious autocracy, deaf to pleas for reform, characterised by a vengeful nationalism, vindictive to minorities but convinced of a holy Orthodoxy, is exactly what seems to be on offer to Russia today. *Plus ca change?*

Or take China. In his study of *The Tyranny of History*, W.J.F. Jenner's theme was that China's extreme deference to history and authority under an all embracive Confucian code was what had stifled China's political, economic and social structures.[1] Though communism was initially seen as a liberation from this suffocating past, in fact its hierarchy has simply replicated it with an even more ruthless repressiveness. For this regime to see hope in the revival of a value system which is at the root of the problem is, though convenient in some respects, utterly disingenuous. The real need is for creative freedom for individuals and minorities to be able to express their own identities – something the present regime wholly discounts. So again the moral vacuum is filled with more of the same from the past, as an attempted solution to a crisis in values.

When Mr Cameron makes his appeal to the Bible and a Christian heritage, it gives the impression of a shared, consensual past that has now been lost. Nothing could be further from the truth when we look at the detail. The very origin of the King James Bible is a case in point, as an attempt to impose some order on a chaotic state of religious turmoil. The Reformation had usurped the established

---

1. W. Jenner. *The Tyranny of History: The Roots of China's Crisis* (Penguin, 1992).

moral authority of the Catholic Church, which had reigned unchallenged for over a millennium. In its place it appealed to the Bible, *sola scriptura,* as the supreme arbiter of moral affairs, a challenge that the Catholic Church vigorously contended: it was not for nothing that the Bible's early translators and proponents were burnt at the stake as heretics. It was a controversy which reduced much of Europe to war-torn desolation in the seventeenth century and, within a generation of his publication, King James's son would have his head on a block, in the hands of disputatious Puritan zealots. Curiously, one thing that spurred these zealots was the sense that a moral vacuum had opened up in the country and that, according to Thomas Hooker, 'God is going from England,' thanks to the resurgence of Catholic practices.[2]

Violent controversy rumbled on across the eighteenth century, as various states vied to impose their own version of moral authority, *cuius regio eius religio.* In doing so, the aristocracy and establishment found the Bible to be a useful tool, not only in imposing *their* authority but shoring up privilege: there seemed no conflict then between biblical morality and, for example, the most appalling trade in human slavery ever organised by man for the most obscene selfish profit. If a Christian country could countenance such a trade, then it is not immediately obvious why the Bible should be a useful tool now to challenge the obscene profits of commercial bankers trading on human misery. Similarly, if we are going to appeal to biblical authority, will that include, as in the USA, the denial of evolution, or, as in some African states, homophobic legislation which criminalises consensual human relationships? As Mr Cameron always likes to be very clear about things, we need to be very clear about this also.

On closer inspection one soon realises what a siren call this appeal to biblical morality really is and how soon controversy – such as that which has riven the Church of England – opens up. Yet, as a sign of just how difficult the alternative has been to digest, or even understand, when Bishop John Robinson made passing reference to such changes in *Honest to God,* it caused a national uproar. Another fifty years on and his statement of the (to him) obvious – that, 'Above all,

---

2. M. Bragg, *The Book of Books: The Radical Impact of the King James Bible 1611–2011* (Sceptre, 2011).

confidence has gone in the type of supernaturalistic ontology to which Christian theology in its classical presentations has been attached' – is still not at all obvious to many. The fear remains of an inevitable moral vacuum opening up, once traditional beliefs are abandoned and the suspicion that once again, 'God is going from England.'

By the nineteenth century, another voice had entered into the controversy: that of secularism. This had the temerity to assert that morality and values were not necessarily dependent on a religious context: that books and blocks of stone did not fall from heaven inscribed with moral commands, but were in fact the human creations of all too human prophets. If the conceit of human inventiveness and imagination was in reality the 'truth' from the past, then why not new, similarly imaginative prophets for the present? It was for failing to grasp the implications of this that Nietzsche berated the 'English flatheads'. But in doing so he was unfairly dismissive of genuinely seminal writers like George Eliot, who were exploring the nature of a new naturalistic basis of morality, which had very different foundations from the previous religious, heteronomous morality of old. It was the achievement of French thinkers such as Durkheim and the founders of sociology to show that moral rules are shaped by society, under the pressure of collective needs. The problem was how, in the wake of extinguished consensual beliefs, to prevent society collapsing into anomic chaos under the weight of conflicting individual demands.

Neither have the new naturalistic or secular moral experiments been without their problems. In her searing account of life in Stalin's work camps of the new socialist regime in the frozen wastes of Siberia, Yevgenia Ginzburg relates an incident when the camp commander lined up his *zeks* (prisoners) and asked them to feel free to express what they really thought about the new order of things.[3] After some hesitation one haggard old man, a former professor of history, had the temerity to speak out saying that never in history had such a mendacious and brutal regime ever been devised by man. The response, typically, was a bullet in the head. Meanwhile, on the other side of the continent, the Lithuanian poet Czeslaw Milosz, reflecting

---

3. Y.Ginzburg, *Within the Worldwind* (1981).

in *The Captive Mind* on the fate of his countrymen under the jack boot of Nazism – which saw a previously civilised people eking out a hunter-gatherer existence in the forests as scavenging bands – and then in the iron grip of the Soviets, he summarised 'the fate of twentieth century man as identical with that of a cave man living in the midst of powerful monsters.'[4]

Yet, curiously, it is in those ancient caves that the glimmerings of an answer to the problem of our moral vacuums is to be found. In the hundreds of thousands of years that constituted the Stone Age, survival depended on being part of a group. It was over these countless millennia – so palaeo-anthropologists tell us – that the social bonds, which alone enabled human survival, were imprinted deep within our psyche: cooperation, sharing, fairness, care for the infirm, respect for nature – these are the moral sentiments that underpin all human activity. Even when over-ridden by 'civilised' ambitions and religious aspirations, they remain as a challenging 'conscience'. It is just such traits which also enabled people to survive even the most ruthless of regimes and brutal times of modern civilisation.

It is therefore not a surprise that when the collapse of the Soviet Union came, it was precisely as a result of the cumulative force of sentiments expressed by such movements as *Solidarnosc* (Solidarity), or in the vast throngs in Wenceslas Square, jangling their keys and calling time on the discredited regime of deception, corruption, and brutality which favoured only the privileged few. It was into the moral vacuum that had opened up at the heart of modernity that new leaders spoke. 'Love, friendship, mercy, humility and forgiveness lost their depth and dimension,' proclaimed Vaclav Havel when he articulated a revolutionary form of non-violent opposition called 'living in truth' – as also did Lech Walesa and Alexander Solzhenitsyn. 'We have learned not to believe in anything, not to care about one another,' he told his compatriots. In this we hear the voice of the natural values that are embedded in humanity and which not only

---

4. C. Milosz, *The Captive Mind* (Penguin, 1981).

pre-exist any ideological or religious context, even civilisation itself, but also pronounce judgement upon them.

So has it always been. When Herodotus wrote his *Histories* – the first great inquiry into human affairs – he was motivated not just by a desire to understand how the great conflict had arisen between Persia and Greece, a war of the worlds between Asia and Europe, he wanted to understand the human workings that under-pinned them and enabled one to triumph over the other. He was in no doubt about this: that what enabled a handful of small Greek states to defeat a great tyrant was their love of freedom; that collaboration was always stronger than compulsion; that democracy allows for the flourishing of the human spirit and creativity, which will always outwit the despot; that the hubris of the mighty is brought low by an ensnaring fate that works through the humble *plebs* (citizens). These were the timeless lessons that Herodotus discovered and taught. In doing so he reminded us of something which perhaps even Nietzsche overlooked – and which as a classicist he should have known better – that there are no new values. Nor is there need for any: what is needed is clarity as to the values that have always made us truly human.

It is the nature of a democracy that things are arranged by consensual agreement. As in politics, so it is with morality: there is no reason not to believe that mature humans are intelligent enough to devise ways of living suited to their needs and arrived at by consensus, rather than by a constant infantile need to appeal to past authority. Such pragmatism is the basis, for example, of Richard Rorty's social hope.[5] Regardless of *our* particular society, political tradition or intellectual heritage, 'In the end, pragmatists tell us, what matters is our loyalty to other human beings clinging together against the dark.' Our hope is not necessarily in getting things 'right' but our participation in fallible and transitory human projects: for these 'obedience' to permanent, inhuman constraints is not necessary. It is a view, one would have thought, that would appeal to a pragmatist like David Cameron. If there is to be hope, Rorty believes, it lies in the imagination, 'in people describing a future in terms which the past

5. R. Rorty, *Philosophy and Social Hope* (Penguin, 1999); also in G. Calder, *Rorty* (Weidenfeld and Nicolson, 2003).

did not use.' By this he is referring to the need for *horizontal* relationships between individuals and groups – characterised by the ongoing description and re-description of relationships – rather than the *vertical* relationship of master and subject, of overpowering metaphysical 'superstructures', which bear down on the defenceless individual.

To some this may appear as a recipe for chaos and anarchy, a vacuum: it is this that still seems most subversive and objectionable to those who claim power over humanity. Yet, as scientists now tell us, vacuums are never empty – just full of what we do not properly understand: they too take on the features of their environment and allow for new possibilities. So it is with moral vacuums – they are full of those deep human instincts which give rise to the world in which we live. Their structures come and go, and it was perhaps the greatest failing of a thinker like Nietzsche to focus too much on the solitary individual – like himself – and individual creative endeavour, rather than the field of play that binds us all together: mastering our own life does not necessarily entail mastering everyone else's – this is how the 'superman' came to be contorted into a monster. The antidote is the ancient, ingrained values of humanity that can exercise a cohesive force. One the earliest on record to understand this was Nietzsche's iconic prophet, Zarathustra. One of the few seemingly genuine teachings that have come down to us from him is the exhortation to 'good thoughts, good words, good deeds.'[6] It is this that lay at the heart of his moral revolution, even if later smothered by ritual and hierarchical accretions: it is this that can still fill our moral vacuums.

---

6. P. Kriwaczek, *In Search of Zarathustra: The First Prophet and the Ideas that Changed the World* (Weidenfeld & Nicolson, 2002).

CHAPTER 12

Spirituality and Sensuosity

Getting beyond the conflict of body and spirit dualism

There are some moments in life that stay with you for ever. They reverberate and return unbidden, often years after but as fresh as at the outset. A modern term for this is 'flashbacks'. Often they are associated with trauma – but not necessarily. For me one such moment took place many decades ago whilst idly browsing among library shelves – actually it was in a Benedictine monastery whilst on a pre-ordination retreat. You don't get much less traumatic than that.

Perhaps it was the unusual title that caught my eye but I picked up a book by Charles Davis entitled *Body as Spirit*.[1] From that moment, as I began to read, I was rooted to the ground. An hour later I was still reading, engrossed, and when I did walk out of the library the world seemed a different place.

For those who have never heard of Charles Davis he was a brilliant theologian and lucid communicator, a doyen of the renewal movement, which was sweeping through the Catholic Church in the 1960s in the wake of Vatican Council II. Then came a thunderbolt: he left the church and got married. For some this was the ultimate apostasy, which merely underlined the perils of questioning traditional orthodoxy. For others it was symptomatic of the problem at the heart the Church, and indeed any religious system: how does it relate to the world.

Perhaps this book was Davis's answer. But it is also an answer that is in need of consideration today at a time of increasing religious ferment and dysfunctional fundamentalisms. In many different faiths adherents grapple with the scepticism of modernity, but also ordinary people are overwhelmed and shocked by the crass materialism and uninhibited greed that now seems to characterise our society.

---

1. C. Davis, *Body as Spirit: The Nature of Religious Feeling* (Hodder & Stoughton, 1976).

Though *Body as Spirit* is a dense and tightly argued book, for me the hinge of it was the second chapter: *The Religious Refusal of the Body*. Davis contrasts the puritan, who sees the body merely as a sensual obstacle to the moral and religious life, and the libertine, who sees the body as a mere instrument of pleasure. But, and here is the unexpected twist, both are denounced for having the same attitude to the body: 'Both, in fact, reject bodiliness. Both fear and repudiate the spontaneous, sensuous *eros* of the body.'

The key to understanding this denunciation is the distinction Davis makes between sensuousness (which I call sensuosity) and sensuality: the former is when we participate in the spontaneous rhythms of the body and are open to the joys and delights of bodily experience and nature; in contrast, sensuality 'is the submission of the body to the driving, straining consciousness of the mind alienated from its bodiliness'; it is what happens when the body is driven by the mind and used as an instrument, either for pleasure, ideological ends or 'super'-natural attainment.

The spiritual significance of bodiliness was exemplified in the recent furore over the loaning of one of the Elgin marbles to the Hermitage Museum in St Petersburg. The statue of Illissos, which personifies the river god, as well as being a masterpiece of craftsmanship, is the epitome of sensuousity. Dr Anna Trofimova, the curator at the Hermitage, commented on the effect of such great sculpture could have on the viewer: 'You look through your eyes but you feel it through your body.'[2] Such is the transformative effect of the sensuous that precedes cognition and changes lives. Encountering such work had changed her life and inspired a career in classical antiquities.

For Davis the dominant materialism of our culture has no love or appreciation of matter, no feel for its organic rhythms or its process of growth and decay: it is purely exploitative. Similarly, the religious consciousness fears the spontaneous rhythms and responses of the body, which are seen as obstacles to the spirit and must be suppressed by a punitive ascetic discipline. Both subject the world

---

2. Quoted in feature article, *The Times*, 5 Dec. 2014.

and body to the calculating mind. Both are exploitative and ultimately destructive.

The alternative is the acceptance of bodiliness as the mediating principle and means of interacting with reality. It is the acceptance of feeling as a sacramental mode, of opening up to and relating with what is before us. Instead of reducing the world to mere physicality or trying to transcend it in favour of some spiritual ideal, it is being in touch with the world through the poetic, imaginative and sensuous faculties. As Davis writes: 'To rediscover bodiliness will be to rediscover our openness to reality.'[3]

To some all this may have strong echoes of D.H. Lawrence; linking spirituality with sensuosity will appear problematic. It might even be annoying that I am making up the word 'sensuosity' to steer beyond mere sensuality to something different – that the spirit reveals itself *through* the body and the world of the senses. This is a challenging navigation.

It is a navigation which the philosopher Martin Buber advances in his famous work *I and Thou*, the purpose of which is to help us to rediscover the meaning of the spirit in the modern world. For him this can only be understood through human relationships: 'Spirit is not in the I, but between I and You'. This is not to be understood in some abstract, theoretical sense but in actual bodily engagement or encounter: 'Whoever stands in a relationship, participates in an actuality'[4]

Such is the spiritual stature of Buber as a teacher that he stands to our times almost as one of the great Old Testament prophets stood to theirs. And it is not without note that he recaptures something of that original understanding of 'spirit' as a powerful, experienced force: an 'identifiable *something*' that brings about a relationship. For Buber it is only here that we can discover a meaningful understanding of the divine, the 'Eternal Thou'.

Nor is it without note that the most challenging, 'problematic' book of the Old Testament is the most sensuous, *The Song of Songs*.

---

3. Davis, *ibid.* p. 53.
4. M. Buber. *I and Thou* (Scribners, 1970), p. 113.

That a poem of such overwhelming erotic fantasy could be understood as such in such a sacred context has always been anathema to some. But there it is. A hymn of lyrical sensuosity, literally at the heart of the Bible. Open a Bible at random in the centre and the odds are you will find an invitation to the beloved leaping out of the page, 'Before the dawn wind rises, before the shadows flee, turn, my beloved, be like a gazelle, a young stag on the mountains.'[5]

In fact it is interesting to note that originally in the Hebrew culture of the Bible the spirit was a very tangible thing: generally it had the same meaning as wind, *ruach,* or breath, *neshma.* Only later did these very observable phenomena gradually lose their realistic roots in theological discourse to become something altogether more abstract, so that in time the spirit had no substance at all: as the theologian Lloyd Geering observed, 'It has become a purely abstract term that has no external referent. It continues in use as a frozen metaphor from a now obsolete worldview, and its only possible meaning is a metaphorical or symbolic one.'[6]

This more traditional 'religious' alternative to the body and senses is suspicious of genuine feelings, particularly 'the blind stirring of love' – as that acclaimed 'spiritual' work, *The Cloud of Unknowing,* would have it. As a consequence, Davis writes, 'Much religion is neurotic, inasmuch as it serves the devious purposes of a divided or enclosed self.' The dualistic division of body and soul becomes schizoid and the neurotic personality avoids reality and protects itself by constructing an unreal, sublimated world: *Noli me tangere,* (touch me not).

And it is not just a religious issue but one it shares with modernity. One of the most disturbing trends of those growing up in the world today is that they are not in fact growing up in the world at all but in a carefully contrived artificiality. This now encompasses significant numbers of people in society as a whole, as well as those within religious or dogmatic communities. Welcome to the world of cyberspace with which modernity increasingly beguiles us. Just as the religious, ideological world frustrates the natural spirit, so does modern

---

5. *Song of Songs,* 2:17.

6. L. Geering, *Reimagining God* (Polebridge, 2014),ch. 13: 'Tomorrow's Spirituality'.

technocracy. It creates an all-embracing virtual world, which like a vampire draws the living blood out of those it ensnares.

Interaction with the natural world is increasingly remote and mediated – either by technology or ideology. What may at first appear as polarities – religion and technology – have some remarkable affinities. The Cloud of Unknowing of spiritual questers is complemented by the Cloud Knowhow of cyber space; ecstatic 'out of body' experience is now more easily available through the gaming consol. Adam Lanza, emerging from his cyber-cellar to shoot a score of children at his local school at Sandy Hook, or the jihadist emerging from his Koranic-induced miasma in the bowels of our cities to perpetrate atrocities, are like characters from Dostoyevsky's 'underground': in fact the distinctive characteristic of the 'other world' of his 'underground man' is that, isolated and introverted, he cannot 'feel'; disgruntled and detached he epitomises the disembodied spirit.[7]

The consequences of such a world were apparent to the psychoanalyst Eric Fromm, as he reflected on our increasingly dysfunctional society in the wake of the Nazi cataclysm: 'Freedom to create and to construct, to wonder and to venture, such freedom requires that the individual be active and responsible, not a slave or well-fed cog in the machine ... if social conditions further the existence of automatons, the result will not be the love of life but love of death.'[8] Creativity, the love of life, arises from the sensuous engagement with the world and others; its rejection entails destruction.

If Fromm were writing today, instead of using the word 'automatons' he might well use 'autistic', that pathological withdrawal into the self. For reasons not clearly understood, this distressing condition seems to be increasingly a feature of modern life. It is surely related to the dramatic change in human lifestyles. Professor Michael Depledge, an Environment Agency chief scientist, notes that the move to cities has been accompanied by an 'incredible rise in depression and behavioural abnormalities', which has similarities to the suffering of wild animals held in captivity.

---

7. F. Dostoyevsky, *Notes From Underground* (Penguin).
8. E. Fromm, *The Heart of Man* (Harper and Row, 1964).

From our long evolutionary history it seems that our brains are hard-wired to feel at peace in the countryside but confused in cities. Recent research (by Dr Ian Frampton of Exeter University) suggests the brain can become overwhelmed in processing visual complexity associated with urban landscapes, in contrast to a natural environment that reduces stress and lowers brain activity, allowing a sense of peace to prevail.[9] Similarly a National Trust report warned of a 'nature disorder deficit' – essentially, children becoming alienated from the outdoors by today's risk averse, screen-addicted society.[10] These are profound lifestyle changes which raise further questions of how we best function as humans; of how our bodies and senses must be allowed to develop if our living spirit is to thrive.

For the ancient Greeks a sound mind in a sound body was an ideal to aspire to. The statue of Illissos exudes its spirit through a body of stone; whilst Illissos reclines in languor, we are ill at ease with ourselves. It seems that we have struggled ever since, frustrated both by our religious beliefs and technological inventiveness. We struggle to live in harmony with ourselves, we even struggle to live in the world with all its sensuous allure. In our own time the suicide bomber has become the ultimate expression of this struggle, of the separation of body and spirit, of the contempt for both the body and the world, of the love of death rather than life. Perhaps the insight of Charles Davis can help us to address this situation and guide us to a more genuinely human spirituality.

---

9. Quoted in *The Independent*, 11 Dec. 2013. It is only in our own time that the majority of humanity has become urban based, increasingly in vast, multi-million urban conglomerates or mega-cities. This also is an aspect of modernity which, as so often, is paradoxical, for though cities have been synonymous with civilisation from the outset and the bearers of progress, their history has been one of unsustainability and destruction. Even our largest and most successful cities, like Mexico City, London or Dubai, teeter perilously on the brink of organisational chaos and environmental unsustainability – the threat of what the archaeologist Ronald Wright has called 'the progress trap' in his brilliant summation of the city in history, *A Short History of Progress* (Canongate, 2004).
10. National Trust, *Natural Childhood,* Report 2013.

III

HERE AND NOW

CHAPTER 13

Ancestral Presences

How the past shadows our present

I awake with a start. As I look out of the bedroom window a brilliant full moon is shining on the frozen landscape. It is the winter solstice and -11 C. The view is both appealing and disturbing, for the moon is very low on the horizon in an unusually northerly quarter, as happens at the winter solstice. But more disconcertingly, in the dream from which I have just awoken, I have been left with a very clear and urgent, if somewhat bizarrely phrased, question: 'Can we prophesy the weather?' In my dream I was standing on the stairway of my old school, which led to the Masters' Staff Room, awaiting the geography master so that I could put my question to him. Unfortunately, I awoke before he descended the stairs and I was given no answer. So, what was all that about?

The evening before I had been reading about the impossibility of predicting the weather for more than six days ahead. Perhaps this was part of the background to my dream as even the most sophisticated computers, capable of trillions of computations, are unable to help the forecasters beyond this span. But then I wasn't asked about a 'forecast' but something altogether more elusive: 'prophecy'. The dream seemed to be presenting some deeper, un-phrased concern that had recently been lurking on the fringes of my mind as my life rushes relentlessly on to its biblical span of three score years and ten: how would it end? What would have been its point? Would anything have been achieved or remain as evidence of its passing?

These are indeed far more urgent concerns than the weather; concerns that at a certain time of life confront us all and which certainly no computer programme can ever answer. As I lay partially awake thinking about this, a pattern of life's futures presented itself, the futures that had already unfolded in those who had now passed away – relatives and friends, a grandfather, uncle and father: ancestors. Though each so different and unique, between them all there seemed to be a similarity in the pattern of their lives, that crossed both time and place, bonding generations. Though so different, there was something about these lives that seemed to hold the answer to my question. But what was it exactly?

I thought of my paternal grandfather – a distant figure of whom I have only a vague remembrance, having met him but once briefly as a child before he passed away. He had recently been brought to mind by a TV documentary on the Indian railways, *Tracks of Empire* by John Sergeant, who had stopped off at what had been one of the great railway workshops of the North Indian Railway at Jamalpur. Taking a walk down Queen's Road, on the old colonial estate, he passed the decaying mansions, the residences of what he described as 'the senior engineers' of the railway. He paused outside a house and my heart nearly missed a beat, as I immediately recognised it from an old family photo as being my grandfather's house, the place where my father had spent the first ten years of his childhood. How amazing!

Perhaps even more amazing was how my grandfather came to be there in the first place, as the chief engineer of the Bengal Railways (as it was) at the beginning of the twentieth century. Having grown up in the back streets of a heavily industrialised suburb of Victorian Manchester, Gorton (more recently made famous as the location of the TV series of benefit scroungers in *Shameless*), and begun his career as a metal turner, he did what most do in difficult circumstances: he took advantage of the opportunities that presented themselves and finished up on the outskirts of empire. But after several decades and an unexpected World War – having received a royal award, presented by the Prince of Wales, for his services of building a railway mun-itions supply line from India to Mesopotamia, bridging the mighty Euphrates on its way – he decided he'd had enough of the empire and returned home.[1] He planned to retire on his savings, only for his wife to die of cancer and his savings to disappear with the collapse of the White Star Line in the Great Depression. Undeterred, he took over a back street pub in Salford dockland to make a living. There, helped by my father, an aspiring but unemployed engineer, he started

---

1. The bridge was a smaller version of the majestic Hardinge Bridge, over a mile long, spanning the Lower Ganges near Calcutta and opened in 1912, which he had been involved in constructing.

138

another life, a long way in every sense from the mansion and ten servants of India with its life of deference and privilege.

And the point of this narrative? Who could possibly have foreseen such an outcome or predicted any of its eventualities? For such is life: often tragic, sometimes serendipitous, but always contingent, ever presenting new challenges and offering new opportunities, which, when taken, have ever further unforeseen consequences, for individuals just as much as for empires. And herein lies a pattern, often forgotten or ignored, underlying the adventure of human life.

What part my grandfather played in this adventure may easily have been forgotten – as it is the fate of the generality of countless 'ordinary' lives to be forgotten – were it not for a few fading sepia prints I still have of him, given to me by my father. Seated in phlegmatic demeanour rather than imperial hauteur, he is surrounded by his staff, one of whom, standing at his side, was a languid youth, whom my father remembered as Lal Tata, an apprentice who had come to learn about steel-working. His ambition, which he would subsequently realise, was to open India's first steel works – an ambition that caused derision amongst colonial officials, one even scoffing the steel would be so useless he would be able to eat it. But Tata became one of the founders of what is now India's greatest industrial dynasty, the current owner of what remains of Britain's steel industry and saviour of the beleaguered remnants of our automotive industry.[2] Again, how amazing!

Meanwhile, my grandfather's great bridge over the Euphrates, having been built to supply munitions to troops in the 'Great War for Civilisation' (as it was then called), was subsequently blown to

---

2. The Tata dynasty was founded by Jamsetji Tata, a Parsee Zoroastrian born in 1839 and among the first Western-educated Indians to emerge from the British Raj. His ambition was to use wealth he had amassed from the opium trade with China to build India's own industrial complex. He first used the profits of his China trade in developing the textile industry but then turned his sights on exploiting the rich coal and iron ore deposits that had been discovered in northern India by creating his own steel works. To do this he scoured Europe and America for the latest technologies and finest engineers. His sons were trained to take forward his ambition of what is now not only Indian's biggest and most respected industrial complex but also Britain's largest manufacturer, employing over 60,000 people, and the world's largest family business.

pieces by the Allies in the First Gulf War, together with the plaque that bore his name,[3] obliterated in the process of historical change that swallows the past and individual memory. As a small vignette of how easily this happens, an older cousin, who was also a distinguished surgeon and was previously in Baghdad to advise on the setting up of hospitals under Saddam's regime, when sight-seeing had crossed the bridge and noted with curiosity his own name on the foundation plaque (he was briefly arrested for photographing a military installation): how strange, he thought, only later to find out it was his own grandfather! But is not this the pattern of the all-consuming Moloch of history, swallowing even memory as it goes, the ever changing march of progress which leaves but ashes of a scarce remembered past?

For what of the ancient Babylonians, and all the empires that followed? Typically, there is a story of endless conflict and devastation, of great cities reduced to smouldering ruins and whole peoples decimated and displaced: Babylon (now Baghdad), Nineveh (now Mosul), Phoenicia (now Gaza), Aleppo ... each city and state rising on the ashes of its predecessor to be reduced to ashes once more – all ravaged, then as now, in a vortex of violence. Such is the 'birthplace of civilisation'; such is the 'law' of progress and change. Yet this is the pattern of civilisation, Did not the philosopher Nietzsche say: 'We build our cities on the slopes of Mount Vesuvius'? The myth of self-transcendence becomes one of self-destruction. Then one realises that this was not just 'then' but is 'now'. This is also a pattern and the same challenge confronts us now. And insofar as 'progress' is the hallmark of modernity, is this also not a myth?

From what I can gather, my grandfather had no great purpose or sense of mission in life other than to get by on his wits, in which he more than amply succeeded. How different would be the life of a maternal uncle – whom again I only briefly met once towards the end of his life – who also went to India, at the same time, but unknown to him, as my grandfather was leaving. He went as a missionary, fulfilling a boyhood dream and becoming the rector of a prestigious college in Jaffna, Ceylon (as it was then). It was a place of

---

3. The Hardinge Bridge was bombed during the civil war of 1971 but subsequently repaired and still used.

dreams, little short of paradise; sun-soaked tropical lands befitting the lotus eaters, with wonderful people. Yet, despite his dedication, and that of many others like him, the outcome was entirely unforeseen – even, unimaginable. From his letters home, towards the end of his life he seemed to sense a portending storm of political discontent, a growing disaffection amongst educated Tamils and the inability of the state to satisfy the aspirations of an educated minority amongst the majority Sinhalese. His life work had been their advancement but he could never have imagined the subsequent brutal civil war that would utterly devastate the place he loved and give the twenty-first century one of its most terrifying icons – the suicide bomber. So noble ideals led to nihilism.

Fortunately for my uncle, he died before the cataclysm and the paradise was lost. But, again, who could possibly have predicted such outcomes? Neither the highest ideals and aspirations nor the pragmatic needs of survival necessarily deliver their promised intent; imperial dreams turn to ashes, paradise becomes a waste land. A pattern seems to replicate itself; two very different lives in every way, my grandfather and uncle, but sharing a deeper homology in the unexpected outcome that could never have been predicted.

And this is what I have found within my own life. Like my uncle, I too set off with missionary zeal, if not as far afield at least with similar intent, becoming a member of a religious order. In the inner city parish where I eventually became resident, I was involved with all kind of dreams, ambitious regeneration schemes, even receiving a national award for the development of community enterprises presented by the Prince of Wales. I remembered my grandfather receiving his award and thinking, 'Snap!'– well, almost. But then it all came to nothing. The parish itself now represents a wilderness, as most of the houses have been cleared in yet another regeneration programme and the parishioners dispersed. Even the great basilica and parochial buildings, which had been the focus of so many dreams, have been abandoned and the church become an Asian banqueting centre. How utterly bizarre and unforeseen, yet within my life was there not, again, something of that ancestral pattern?

Before this happened I had left the parish and ministry. In the end I felt I could no longer believe in its aspirations and, perhaps like my grandfather, decided I had had enough of a way of life and returned home to care for my aging father. It was then I began to think more frequently of his presence and like him, in the interests of survival, took on an altogether different mode of life from that of clerical privilege and deference, getting a job as an operative with a Home Improvement Agency. I found myself allocated to the Gorton area of Manchester – where my grandfather's family had settled nearly two centuries previously – visiting the houses of the elderly, doing all sorts of small jobs: fixing taps and locks, repairing gates and cupboards, toilets and windows. Such are the basics of life.

Yet there was always a sense of something more, something beyond, something 'other'; that in fact the pattern of my life was mirroring that of others. This first forcibly struck me when, before his death, I recorded the life of my father. So much of the contingency of his life seemed to anticipate my own. After his death, what also surprised me was how often small things seemed to in- dicate something 'other' as when, for example, I needed some fitting for an awkward job. I could go to the rows of old tea boxes which my uncle used to send from Ceylon, then filled with choice teas, but which still line my (and previously my father's) workshop shelf – filled now with all sorts of engineering detritus he had accumulated. More often than not the needed item would be the first thing I spotted as I opened a box, as if it had been given, selected and proffered to me. The frequency with which this happens sometimes startles me. And with it, again, comes a sense of that ancestral presence; a presence that in varied ways makes life possible.

And I am constantly surprised by what this has enabled me to achieve, as if by their shadowed presence patterns were being pre- arranged. In the turmoil of life we can become oblivious of such things, except, perhaps, at those rare moments of quietude, as at a solstice when time turns back on itself in a reflective pause, or when we lie half-awake to the world. At such moments we seem to see into the life of things and experience, 'A motion and a spirit, that impels all thinking things, all objects of all thought. And rolls through all things' (*Lines Written above Tintern Abbey* – Wordsworth). What then, we may ask, does life prophesy? As I consider the outcome of their lives, in their very perturbations, ancestors seem to be teaching much about life. They challenge us to a deeper understanding of the past and of the present. Isn't this 'prophecy'? For prophecy is not looking 'out' but looking 'into'; not into the future but into the present, to understand its meaning and the heart of things. It is the power of reflection to recognise a pattern and that among those deeper murmurings of tragedy and ambition, affection and kindness there is a presence that will continue.

Remembrance and respect for the ancestors who have gone before us is not now something that has much place in our postmodern and frenzied age, focused as it is on immediate goals and short term achievement. Just as many don't have time to pay much attention to the winter solstice, neither do they give much thought to the ancestral presence. Yet both are powers that shape our lives – the former our natural world and the latter our social world. If all this seems too remote and obscure, then we are diminished. Though we may not notice, they are there, the solstice in the cycle of the rebirth of life and the ancestors in the possibilities that life now offers to us, their latest offspring.

Like the ancestors, the whole concourse of history remains shrouded and soon forgotten, but nonetheless effective in its presence and undiminished in its power. Like the ancient henge monuments or the Moa of the Easter Island, as we draw away from them they take on altogether greater significance and their proportions dominate the horizon of life. In some cultures their domain is defined by enigmatic notions such as the 'shadow-walkers' or 'shape-shifters' that shroud the present in unsuspecting ways. They remind us that the present is a product of the past, that its 'play' takes place on the pre-structured stage of their creation.

As we peer with oracular insight into the kaleidoscope of events with their patterns of contingency, we confront the unpredictability of the present. Yet instability (or 'dissipative structures', in the jargon of evolutionary biology, which create order out of chaos) is what makes new life possible. Above all else it characterises the unpredictability of 'modernity', which, in turn, is simply a more elaborate way of saying 'the present moment'. Its mutations and transformations are reminiscent of the kaleidoscope I once had as child. One nudge and the brilliant pieces re-form to shape yet another shimmering pattern, prompting gasps of amazement; each uniquely different, never to be recaptured. Yet the pieces remained the same and the patterns discernibly similar, all of a piece. So with each generation, unique yet the patterns of life reshape themselves in recognisable ways. Individual lives and social life carry the patterns of the past with them in their structural homologies. As we struggle to understand the process, the novelty always surprises.

Within this world of evanescence and unpredictability, is it not surprising that people have increasingly sought for their certainties in the past? The confidence in progress, that characterised 'modernity', has for many been replaced by uncertainty and the ideologies of fundamentalism, which seek reassurance and guidance from the past. My understanding of the lives of my ancestors is that the past cannot provide those certainties; their lives were as full of uncertainties as ours. The ancestors do not provide answers, they are simply a presence. They give a sense of familiarity, of belonging. They shadow the present in a way that shadows on the landscape give it depth, from which we can take shelter in the light of the midday sun – whilst continuing on our own journey.

If we have any purpose in life, it will be subsumed in the fact that one day we too will become ancestors. If there is a destiny that shapes our ends, this will be it – to make way for others. But it is in what we do now that future worlds will be shaped, serendipitously perhaps, though through their contingency this eludes us now.

But what, in the end, is the answer to my question? Can we prophesy the weather – or anything else in life? And the answer, as so often in the way of oracular utterance, is a paradox. The weather is simply present, ever changing but recognisable by the same repetitious forms in which patterns can be discerned. We prophesy the present through patterns from the past, which give us confidence to face the future. The shadowed past shapes the present and from it we can learn something of the shape of reality, even of the future – if we have the prescience to discern it.

Such thoughts tumble through my mind as the solstice dawns, but time now to get up. The moon has gone, the sun has arisen; time to get on with life.

CHAPTER 14

Life's Mystery

How modern thought is challenging our understanding of life

At the centre of every life is the desire for coherence, meaning, pur-pose... It is a web woven between two poles of an ellipse – the inner personal order and the outer, grander order of nature. The traditional purpose of religion is to mediate a framework of the construction of a persuasive order or context of understanding.

In the West this has been the traditional role of the church(es). It presents an orthodoxy as a standard by which all things can be assess-ed; a fixed body of knowledge and law mediated by the institutionally accredited figure – the priest – who also enacts the ritual procedures of order. So it has been in various ways since the dawn of recorded history: but no longer.

The tide of supernatural causality as an explanation of the natural order has consistently withdrawn in the face of an ever more awe-some understanding of nature. Through a seemingly endless process of deference, myths of origin have become remote functional hypo-theses. In the personal realm, the understanding of the brain/mind and its evolution unmasks those projections of symbolic creativity which we had once taken as revelatory of some other power: God.

Now, for the first time – in our own time – we have the essential elements of a coherent cosmological view of man as a phenomenon within a majestic natural order, an order which is simply be(com)ing. It is a view which cannot be reconciled with the previous foun-dational understanding of Western culture implicit in Plato's ideal world, with its abstract metaphysics of presence, nor with the 'otherness' of monotheism. The new dogmas are of relativity and uncertainty, our world synthetic, pragmatic and technocratic.

Such an understanding has been growing since at least the seven-teenth century and has often been characterised as a conflict between belief and unbelief, the forces of religion and secularism. But if it once had this aspect, this is now no longer properly descriptive. What we have witnessed is the birth of a new total explanatory system, which simply discards the old polarities of belief and unbelief. A new spirituality has emerged focused on life: life in its totality, with a reverence for all that is; an attention to beings rather than being.

The meaning of 'being' is crucial: not the abstracted, personified, deified Being – the ever threatening tyranny of an ideal, which even in its secularised opposite became the tyranny of ideology – but 'be-ing' as simply gratuitous givenness/givingness in transience; the be(com)ing which is no-'thing' in itself but the context of existence. The recognition, at last, that we need not run away from the reality of time, finitude or transience for the illusion of an absolute eternity or certainty.

A different understanding of be-ing brings with it a whole new spirituality of openness, acceptance and gratitude for the present moment. This sense has often existed on the mystical fringes of established religions but was deemed subversive of hierarchical order. Now it is just right for a global democratic order with its egalitarian creativity.

All this is not so much subversion as supersession: past forms no longer satisfy. Vocation becomes the willingness to search, the journey of self-discovery rather than conformity. We are to be the artists of our own life in a future as yet unknown and for which the past no longer provides a guide.

In one of his writings Isaiah Berlin, the distinguished historian of ideas, reflected on the pathway which had brought him to his present state of life: things happened and choices had been made which had created the present.[1] It could have been different. Other events, other choices would have created a different pathway and a different present. For all of us this is true: our present could have been different.

As it is, our present is different by virtue of the unique path we have travelled. Every path is distinctive and deserves respect. In this century of totalitarian ideologies, which have set out to crush deviation, this is important. There are distinctive ways but there is no definitive way. A fundamental fact of humanity is, as Berlin termed

---

1. Cf. J. Gray, *Isaiah Berlin* (Collins, 1995).

it, 'incommensurability' – people, societies, cultures, are different, not necessarily better or worse, just different, profoundly distinctive: incommensurable.[2] It is this that renders modern liberal societies so unstable and fissiparous but also gives them their vitality and appeal – people can be themselves: individuals.

To some, if not many, this is a frightening – even an intolerable – thought that is seen to undermine order and stability. To live with difference suggests the possibility of the relativity of values. More generally it provokes a fear that is reflected in modern 'fundamentalism' that strives for conformity in its inability to understand that convictions are not necessarily certainties. Yet everything in creation suggests this reality; that everything has the potentiality to become *itself*, most fully, in quite a unique way.

This theme was explored by Marcel Proust in what is often considered to be the greatest novel of the twentieth century: À *la Recherche du temps perdu* – the remembrance of times past, but which we seek again; even the translation is uncertain and ambiguous.[3] Again different pathways are explored, by the narrator, 'Marcel', and the possibilities life presents. At one point at the beginning of the novel he wanders down Swann's Way and is overwhelmed by the beauty of the hawthorn bush in flower, each of its flowers shaped with such unique perfection.

It is strange how a passage from literature can 'open one's eyes' to reality, as if for the first time. I subsequently remember observing the many hawthorn bushes that surround a nearby golf course and in May annually unfold a breath-taking bridal display of shimmering white blossom. Looking closely at each flower, one is amazed to see, that while all are recognisably similar, each is quite unique. There may be similarity, but there is no sameness in creation, for everything is unique. Looking at a single hawthorn flower, one has a sense of being in the presence of a *mysterium tremendum* – the mystery of life.

The natural order is profoundly 'individual', but also embracive, ecumenical and empathetic, to which I too can contribute something unique. I may not bring anything into the world or take anything

2. I. Berlin, *Four Essays on Liberty* (OUP, 1969).
3. M. Proust, *Remembrance of Things Past,* trans. C.K. Scott Moncrieff (Penguin, 1983).

from it, but I, as we all can, have the power to contribute something of my/ourself in a way that will enrich the world and which only I can contribute.

I am part of an unfinished world, which invites me to go on living. It is a world of which I become conscious, a world whose reality transcends its corporeality, a world to which my mind is the key – the key to life's greatest mystery: the mind. It was to this mystery that Edwin Schrödinger, one of the twentieth century's most outstanding scientists, sought to draw attention in his essay, 'Mind and Matter'.[4] What he sought to challenge was the principle of 'objectivation' underlying all Western science since its origins among the Greeks: that there is an objective or real world outside us, upon which we can look merely as detached observers. From Democritus to Descartes and Kant this obsession with 'the-thing-in-itself' had proved to be continually elusive.

It is elusive simply because it is an illusion: we are not external to the world, we are part of it. Even more challenging, 'The world is given to me only once, not one existing and one perceived'.[5] We are in a relational embrace with the world; there is no barrier between the two polarities of subject and object, for they are one, just as there are no polarities between the mother and child, they are one nursing relationship. The universe is not just a collection of objects but a communion of subjects; life not an endless interaction of discrete entities, like snooker balls bouncing off each other, but an intercommunion which provides the basis not of conformity but for the emergence of difference.

This 'relational' view of the universe and of life has now become the basis of a new understanding of the cosmos. As cosmologist Lee Smolin explained, 'the desire to understand the world in terms of a naïve and radical atomism, in which elementary particles carry forever fixed properties, independent of history or the shape of the universe, perpetuates a now archaic view of the world.'[6] It is a world

---

4. E. Schrödinger, 'Mind and Matter' in *What is Life?* (Cambridge University Press, 1938/1992).
5. W. Moore, *Schrödinger: Life and Thought* (CUP, 1989), p. 437 for a discussion of the 'world view of science.'
6. L. Smolin, *The Life of the Cosmos* (Phoenix, 1997), p.21.

view associated with Newton and the desire for an 'absolute' point of view, such as Schrödinger spoke of in relation to the underlying 'myth' of Western science.

In contrast and by strange coincidence, as Smolin points out, the alternative to the Newtonian view was championed by Newton's own contemporary and great polymathic rival, Leibniz. In contrast to Newton's view of absolute properties, the alternative view may be called relational – that the properties of things are not fixed absolutely with respect to some unchanging background but arise from interactions and relationships. As a result, as Smolin goes on to explain, 'the world must be understood to be the result of processes of self-organisation, and not just the reflection of fixed and eternal natural law.'[7] In this dynamic view of the universe, life is not just an improbable accident but part of its very structure.

The botanist Rupert Sheldrake takes this understanding a stage further in challenging the tradition of Western science that describes life in narrowly rational and mechanistic terms.[8] His core contention is that the paradigm of thought by which we understand the universe has changed from being a mechanistic model to one of a living organism, which is organised by fields of energy. This moves us on from the whole reductionist view of bits of inanimate 'stuff' interacting, to a more gracious view of nature being animated by 'fields' of energy, which have taken the place of the old idea of 'soul' as an organising principle. Fields of energy are now at the heart of the new understanding of physics.[9]

Some attempt to dismiss all this as 'pseudo-science'. But in fact it is simply offering a more 'spiritual' view of science. There is nothing inherently more irrational in this than the great irrational mystery that typifies our universe. If there has been a change over the last thirty years, it is in a greater willingness to recognise this; areas of enquiry have opened up even greater areas of ignorance. For example Paul Davies (director of the tellingly named *Beyond Centre for Fundamental*

7. Smolin, *ibid.* p.17.
8. R. Sheldrake. *The Science Delusion: Freeing the Spirit of Enquiry* (Coronet, 2012).
9. F. Capra, *The Tao of Physics: An Exploration of the Parallels between Modern Physics and Eastern Mysticism* (Flamingo, 1991). Also E. Laszlo, *The Creative Cosmos: A Unified Science of Matter, Life and Mind* (Floris Books, 1993).

Concepts in Science at Arizona State University) thinks that a 'proper understanding' of dark energy 'will probably require new physics',[10] whilst theoretical mathematician John Barrow thinks our inherently anthropic limits of perspective will always prevent us from comprehending the symmetries that underlie the great forces of nature.[11]

Perhaps it is too demanding for us to grasp this reality or understand our true place within the fabric of the universe; to take stock of the fact that the localisation of personality or consciousness inside the body is symbolic of our localisation in the universe. Certainly, the quantum world, which Schrödinger's seminal work helped to define, recognises no such 'localisation'. It now seems more natural for us to assume that the mind is merely the effect of certain neurological functions; a position which is the obverse of the pre-scientific 'religious' view of the mind (or soul) as something 'given' and the 'real' world, of the gods and celestial powers, as something revealed. Such is the Platonic world view.[12] But the polarity of this 'theological' elliptic is itself a trick of the mind. Nature is one interactive, transactional entity of which we are part: body and spirit are one, the 'spiritual' is one with the world as light is to existence – not shining on the world, but of it and through it.

In a sense all reality contains a revelatory nature, an openness to transcendence; not the polarity of nature and super-nature, but at every point and moment of existence there is a sense of mystery – a mystery that arises not through pure unintelligibility but because things are intelligible, though never wholly so nor in ways we at first expect. Laws and theories can be formulated to a remarkable degree, but they are never conclusive. As in Gödel's famous theorem, every system points beyond itself for verification.[13] In this sense everything that exists is a pointer beyond itself, almost as a sign or sacrament: it

10. P. Davis, *The Cosmic Blueprint: Order and Complexity at the Edge of Chaos* (Penguin, 1995).
11. J. Barrow & J. Silk, *The Left Hand of Creation: The Origin and Evolution of the Expanding Universe* (Penguin, 1995).
12. R. Sheldrake & M. Fox, *Natural Grace: Dialogues in Science and Spirituality* (Bloomsbury, 1996).
13. Cf. C. Clarke, *Reality Through the Looking Glass: Science and Awareness in the Postmodern World* (Floris, 1996).

makes us aware that we are in the presence of greater things, the *mysterium tremendum,* the wholeness/holiness to which we must defer.

Over recent centuries the sense of sacramentality has become increasingly attenuated, not just by secularism but, paradoxically, even previously by religious belief itself. For example, in the Roman Catholic Church for over a millennium there has been an increasing restriction of sacramentality to a few particular, ritual acts (something never so confined in the Eastern Orthodox position), under strictly clerical administration.[14] One could even go so far as to say that sacramentality has been so shrouded in liturgical ritual that it has lost contact with everyday reality: not even the communion wafer is recognisable as bread.

Traditional organised religion, particularly in the West, has been slow to recognise the changes that have been taking place in scientific thinking, just as it has been slow to recognise the threat to the basic life systems of the Earth that have arisen from modern industrialised culture. Ecologist Thomas Berry, himself a Roman Catholic priest, is forthright in his condemnation that throughout the modern period, 'the traditional spiritual leaders – scholars, religious teachers, and social reformers – have been unable to provide sufficient guidance.'[15] For him this failure has arisen because of the failure to recognise that the basic issue is not simply divine-human or inter-human relations but, 'human-Earth relations, and beyond that, relations with the comprehensive community of the entire universe.' For Berry this new story of the universe is our new 'sacred story', though one which few of the traditional spiritual guides have seemed able to accept or even understand: sensitivity to the universe is 'the primary religious mode of being and to ourselves being religious (is) through our participation in the religion of the universe.'[16]

The dualism of scientific thought, which Schrödinger identified as the principle of objectivation underlying Western science since the time of the ancient Greeks, shows itself again here in all its most destructive potency in the traditional attitude to nature as an

---

14. Sheldrake, *ibid.*
15. T. Berry, *The Sacred Universe.* Quoted in Thomas Berry, *Selected Writings on the Earth Community* (Orbis, 2014), p. 81.
16. Berry, *ibid.* p.66.

'externality' to human culture; that nature is simply 'given'. As the ecologist Christian Schwägerl writes, this attitude expresses itself in 'our Western economic system, resting on the assumption that nature is something to exploit, whether as a material resource or as a backdrop for the tourism industry.'[17] It is a paradigm which again has to be set aside, not just so that we can make progress but, this time, so that we may survive.

The revelatory power of reality continues to beat upon our senses, and not just in terms of intelligibility. For everything is in a state of dynamism, a living expression of unimaginable, though restrained, energy and power. We now understand the universe not as a static entity but as a living organism with a life history; even the line between non-life (matter) and life turns out to be an arbitrary one drawn by humans. Instead of speaking about the cosmos we now speak of cosmogenesis. Perhaps the greatest discovery of astronomy in the twentieth century was that of Edwin Hubble in 1929 of the so-called 'red shift', which indicated that the universe was not static but expanding. This new insight transformed everything: it meant that the whole cosmos is in a process of evolution. It was as if it were 'alive', that it had an age and it also had a future.

This understanding required a whole new approach to cosmology and the mystery of life. It was a challenge to which the geologist and priest Teilhard de Chardin attempted to respond. As a Roman Catholic and priest it was Teilhard's ambition to relocate Christianity within this larger framework of thought, over which he rhapsodised and about which he dreamed hitherto unimagined thoughts. For this mystical palaeontologist matter was sacred; nothing could be viewed in isolation, everything part of a cosmic 'plan', of which we were a part and which should inspire a new hymn to the universe from us. His radicalism lay in the complete break with all previous views that divided reality into two polarities, a spiritual world and a physical world; his challenge was the attempt to express spiritual thoughts in scientific language.

Looking back we can see that in some ways he failed: his work was banned as 'unorthodox' by the church, which effectively silenced

---

17. C. Schwägerl, *The Anthropocene – The Human Era and How it Shapes our Planet* (Synergetic Press, 2015).

him for a lifetime; when his work was eventually published, after his death, it was ridiculed by scientists such as Sir Peter Medawar as 'nonsense' and 'bad science'. But what Teilhard did achieve was to present a way of thinking about the world and the universe which was integral, holistic, dynamic and inspiring – that everything is part of a vast cosmogenic process. It was an idea taken up by what is called 'process theology'. As Teilhard himself modestly reflected at the end of his life, 'If I have had a mission to fulfil, it will only be possible to judge whether I have accomplished it by the extent to which others go beyond me...'[18]

As a result of this new understanding of the universe and of matter as energy, it is now possible to see even traditional writings such as the gospels in new light. Essential in the way they present the ministry of Christ is not that he helped us to a greater understanding – as the gnostics would claim – but that he exuded power. We are told in the gospels that in everyday simple acts, 'Power went out through him'. These acts were their own witness but accompanied by a command 'Tell no one'. It is as if there is recognition that power contains a terrible ambivalence: to create and destroy.

The gospels describe power as *exousia* – the power to heal and make whole – but the Romans understood power in quite a different way, as *potestas* – the power to crush, to rule, to dominate, forcing conformity. And it is such power that most appeals to man. In fact one sets itself up as the perfect counterfeit of the other. Interestingly, such was the pivotal point of controversy between so called liberation theologians and the Vatican in the 1980s, over not only the nature of power but who should possess power in the church: the people or the papacy. On such an issue hinged the primal struggle of man, as depicted in the myth of Prometheus, who stole power from the gods, in the form of fire, for his own ends.

The purpose of power is to bring fullness of life. In nature we can observe this constantly at work, but not so easily in society. To achieve this in the human community is the work of therapy, not in any clinical sense but in its original Greek sense of a work (*therapeia*),

---

18. A sympathetic and balanced account of this enigmatic but inspiring thinker is given in L. Geering, *Religious Trailblazers* (St. Andrew's Trust, 1992), ch.4: 'Pierre Teilhard de Chardin: God is Evolving'.

carried out by the one responsible for looking after the household, the *therapon*, so as to create a wholesome environment where the household may be at peace with itself and its ancestral roots. It is in such a state that one comes into the greater 'presence' that lies at the heart of every household, the ancestral gods – the *therapein*, or in Hebrew *teraphim*. Such a 'therapeutic community' is one where each individual grows in their own particular way to realise the potential (*potential*: power) which is uniquely theirs, given only once, otherwise to be lost for ever.

Think of our condition had not Michelangelo or Mozart, Leonardo or Einstein, received and realised their chance. Then think of the frustrated tedium that suffocates the lives of countless millions: such is humanity's greatest loss and waste. The challenge of personal growth and self-fulfilment for the individual is above all else the challenge to grow: virtue – the 'manliness' required of the responsible citizen.

That individual growth only takes place within a vibrant community is something that we have tended to lose sight of in the West. Over the last 150 years an evolutionary view of life has grown up centred almost entirely on individual competitiveness, encapsulated by the phrase 'the survival of the fittest'. But fitness is also about 'fitting in': fitting in to a community or network of relationships is what enables us to survive. Darwin himself recognised 'the contented face of nature', which arises from the harmony, even cooperation, existing between species on many different levels: even trees seem to make way for other species in the shared canopy. This wonderful interactivity is the core thesis of modern ecology and bio-diversity, in particular Gaia theory, which sees the central feature of nature as maintaining a homeostasis between all living things. It is a reality from which humankind cannot exempt itself.[19]

The great cultures and spiritual traditions of the world have always had to struggle with these issues. For the ancient Greeks there were always problems with humankind, in its confused yet limitless ambitions, which only the gods (the embodied powers of nature) could frustrate. The ensuing struggle to achieve domination over

---

19. F. Capra, *The Hidden Connections: A Science for Sustainable Living* (Flamingo, 2002).

nature – often under the guise of 'stewardship' – has led to the subjection of the planet to human needs. Now, with the imminent threat of ecological collapse (ecocide), there is urgent need to recognise we are but a component of a holistic community, in which nature has prior stewardship over us.[20] Eventually the hubristic individual must learn to acknowledge his limits and respect the greater 'Other' and others.

Within the human community this comes about most immediately through personal relations and shared consciousness, arising from a shared language and leading us to understand that, in its deepest sense, reality is a community of being: in the Christian tradition this is expressed in the 'tri-unity' of the Godhead. The sense of struggling to be free from self-frustration or karma is also central to the methods and teachings of Buddhism, which seek to encourage the individual to grow beyond self and focus the mind, on its own spiritual nature and destiny.

The problem for Westernised societies is not only their competitive, material possessiveness, but the confusing plurality of lifestyles and the privatisation of meaning. This makes the individual an unstable entity or 'conversion prone', as the sociologist, Peter Berger, described it, 'liable to fundamental transformations in the course of his career.' A feature which in turn encourages a fundamentalist mind-set of clinging to ever more extreme convictions to compensate for uncertainty.[21]

Ultimately, we grow towards a final point, death. At that point what we have become is given back. It is perhaps this that is most difficult to achieve, for not only must we give up our possessions but we must also surrender our self. It is in this submission we achieve our final end and confrontation with perhaps the most profound paradox of creation: that in the last 'end' we find the clue to the first cause; just as at the outset the artist has an idea of his composition, so we find the true significance of creation not at the beginning but at the end, and that we have contributed to it.

20. Berry, *ibid.* p.177.
21. Cf. D. Zohar & I. Marshall, *The Quantum Society: Mind, Physics and a New Social Vision* (Flamingo, 1994), particularly p.226.

This is what both biological and physical sciences are also beginning to reveal: that there is an enigmatic 'downward causation', which precedes the more obvious emergence of 'upward causation'. This 'teleonomic character of living organisms' is something which the distinguished biologist Jacques Monod reluctantly had to admit, and which seemed to press 'a profound epistemological contradiction' upon him.[22] Similarly, in the realm of quantum theory, Sir Arthur Eddington once wondered – in the light of observations made on the strange behaviour of quantum particles – whether or not a fundamental reconstruction was 'now pressing on us', in which secondary laws (i.e. those concerning general principles) become the basis of our understanding of life and primary laws (those concerning the immediate behaviour of elementary particles) are discarded.[23] In other words the end is implicit in the beginning, the individual is inseparable from the whole.

At this point of paradox and mystery we come back to the point at which we started. That every life is given only once and every path is a unique adventure freely chosen. Upon that journey we have one goal, to discover our self and enable it to come to the fullness of being *(pleroma)*, thereupon to surrender and loose it to return to the eternal presence of creation, from whence it came with so much expectation and to which it contributes a final fullness.

---

22. J. Monad, *Chance and Necessity* (Penguin, 1971). Cf. also P. Davis,. *The Cosmic Blueprint: Order and Complexity at the Edge of Chaos* (Penguin, 1995).
23. Quoted in Davis, *ibid.* p. 175.

CHAPTER 15

Credo: A View of Life

So what was all that about? After decades of living I ask myself: What did I make of it all? Childhood dreams, aspirations and ambitions, anticipations and longings – where did they all lead? What was my destiny? Destiny, as the poet Rilke wrote, is but childhood dreams interpreted in the light of experience.

Generally, the world has been plagued by men – and it is mostly men! – who felt themselves 'called', destined for great things. We look back and create patterns of meaning with which to confront the future. This itself betrays a most fundamental characteristic of humans: we search for meanings, we need to make sense of 'it all'. But how? Chapter 10 quoted George Eliot's little 'parable' in *Middlemarch* that points out how, if we place a lit candle on a scratched, polished steel plate 'the scratches will all seem to arrange themselves in fine series of concentric circles around that little light.'[1] Thus we arrange the events of our lives around the light of our Self. Our meanings gradually coalesce; 'a' meaning subtly becomes transposed into 'the' meaning, having found which we feel content. Thus we deceive ourselves, falling into the trap – the 'ontological illusion' of the medieval scholar St Anselm – that the greatest of ideas cannot but be real. That our destiny is predestined. But in fact our grandiosity remains our own creation.

Another view, a more modern and humbler view of life, was taken by Viktor Frankl, peering at life through the barbed wire fencing of the Auschwitz extermination camp – yes, this is what 'men of destiny', convinced of the greatness of their ideas, create. He saw that we derive meaning in our lives from the small encounters and events of everyday – the 'scratchings' of life – by our attitude.[2]

As Frankl so often watched human life ebb away in the most horrific circumstances, he realised that each day there are three things

---

1. George Eliot, *Middlemarch* (OUP, 1996), ch. 27, p. 248.
2. V. Frankl, *Man's Search for Meaning: An Introduction to Logotherapy* (Hodder & Stoughton, 1964), p. 113.

our existence calls upon us to achieve if we are to find fulfilment and meaning: we must do a deed of generosity or create something of value from our own powers, which itself expresses life's abundance and bounty; we must appreciate something of value such as a work of art or natural beauty which takes us beyond ourselves; we must carry a burden or endure suffering positively, reminding us that life is never easy or to be taken for granted, that our lives are never perfect or 'finished'.

Of these three things I have often thought that being creative is the most important. It is in the act of creating 'something' that we also create our 'self'; we discover or realise something of ourselves and our capabilities of which we were previously unaware. In the art and craft classes that I run for senior citizens I am often struck by how people belittle themselves when a project is suggested: 'Oh, I can't do that' or, 'Oh, I've never done anything like that before', to which I reply 'Good, all the more reason we should try now,' on which, having completed the work they are filled with amazement and satisfaction that they have indeed created something new. I never fail to be amazed at the sense of fulfilment that always accompanies such creative endeavour, not only of satisfaction but self-realisation.

Nor is it just a matter of imposing one's will on materials or working to a preordained idea. The true craftsman will first caress his materials, reflect on their nature and potentiality, work with their grain in a profound respect for what is 'other'. So often, when teaching DIY courses, I have found that problems arise when insufficient thought has been spent on these rather abstract preliminaries. Yet much of the satisfaction comes with the surprise of finding that the materials themselves 'suggest' things, so that the end product is something far more than intended. I remember, for example, once making 'tree men' out of some old logs: it was with surprise and great amusement we saw little 'creatures' emerge from the dead logs each with their own personality. Perhaps it was a similar experience of watching a potter moulding clay figures that gave the writer of the biblical creation story the idea of the creator moulding and drawing forth man from the red earth clay, in Hebrew *adamah*.

If it is from such acts of creativity that we find a new and fuller appreciation of life, then that other great contemporary of Frankl's, Martin Buber, who has already appeared in this book, gives us further insight. For him, 'all living is meeting'.[3] It is in the encounters of daily living with others that we discover ourselves. Every encounter invites a response that should spring from the depths of our personality, this is our '*response*-ibility', which helps to create the person we are, that calls us forth.

Like the craftsman who draws forth something new from his materials, something more than existed before, so for Buber in our meetings with others something new emerges, something transcendent, a spirit which did not previously exist. As Buber wrote, 'Spirit is not in the I, but between I and Thou', it is not like the blood that circulates within me but like the air which we breathe together. For Buber this was the basis of the divine: God is the 'other', we address 'God' whenever we address and respond to a fellow human being.

This is reminiscent of the gospel teaching: 'Where two or three are gathered together in my name, there I am in the midst of them.' There is always a greater 'presence' in human sharing. I have often found this when taking school groups on picnics or on summer camps: I would say, 'Let's put all our food together and share', as did the boy in the gospel story with the loaves and fishes. Always, everyone has more than enough with a sense that in the process of sharing a community has been formed.

These two writers of the twentieth century, Frankl and Buber, give us an insight into how far mankind has travelled in its search for meaning since its remote beginnings. When we look back to the earliest evidence of how man saw his world, some forty millennia ago, we see, in the palaeolithic cave art of southern Europe, a very different understanding.[4] Here a world is portrayed in which puny humans are challenged by the power of its creatures and the natural order. It is a world before morality or deities, before good and evil, in which man tries to create a place for himself through the shamanistic manipulation of natural forces.

Over the millennia humans have undertaken a stupendous spiritual journey which has taken them from shamanism to humanism, from ritual enactment to human engagement, from the amoral order

---

3. A. Hodes, *Encounter with Martin Buber* (Allen Lane, 1972).
4. D. Lewis-Williams, *The Mind in the Cave* (Thames and Hudson, 2002). Also, *Inside the Neolithic Mind* (2005).

of natural survival to the moral sense of common responsibility. It is a journey that saw the creation of powerful elites and hierarchies, the divinisation of natural powers and the creation of the gods, the ritualisation of life and the sacrificial order of intercession, to perhaps the greatest human creation of all, the idea of one all-consuming explanatory power, God – as in 'Abrahamic monotheism': a unitary, all-powerful figure that strides the cosmos for ever, the ultimate male fantasy from pharaohs to fascists! [5]

Such configurations linger on, as does the vestigial tiered cosmos of the cave world with its tripartite division of heaven, world and underworld, its haunting monsters and intermediary spiritual agents, angels or 'soul carriers', and its sense of 'super'-natural endings. But we have now passed on beyond such meanings, even beyond the hypostasisation of good and evil, as simply 'given' realities, to the challenge of human encounters: of what we must do to become humane.

It was only relatively recently, historically, that a moral element was introduced into human religious beliefs, most notably by Zarathustra some four thousand years ago, with his sense of the goodness of creation by one all-powerful being. 'The Good Religion', as his followers call their faith, remembers little of his teaching other than the injunction to practise 'good thoughts, good words, good deeds.' Such was the challenge to traditional ritualism that he was assassinated, stabbed in the back by a *karapan* (priest).[6]

We have now passed on to an understanding of that which binds us – *religio* – and the origin of the word 'religion' is not some universal 'solution' to life, some ideology or dogma, but the human engagement that binds us to each other each day. The greatest sages of ancient Israel, Hillel and Jesus, summed up the essence of their belief and religious tradition in the same way: refrain from that which you would not want others do to you, and do to others as you would have them do to you: 'This is the meaning of the Law and the Prophets.' True religion is that which binds us to each other.

---

5. L. Geering, *Reimagining God* (Polebridge, 2014), ch. 8: 'How Humans Made God'.
6. P. Kriwaczek, *In Search of Zarathustra: The First Prophet and the Ideas that Changed the World* (Weidenfeld & Nicolson, 2002).

How neglected this teaching has been! The prophet Isaiah came to understand the essential quality of divinity as *hesed*: loving kindness. Today we watch on our news bulletins as orthodox Hassidic Jews – whose name derives from *hesed* – rejoice at the shelling of Gaza. So has it ever been. Millenarian attempts in the tenth century Rhineland and southern Europe to revive the Apostolic Life of brotherly love – of which Norbert of Xanten's Pentecostal community at Prémontré was one example – led to their demonisation by the Inquisition of the official church and then their extermination through the Albigensian crusade.[7] It was left to Dostoyevsky's Grand Inquisitor to point out just how dangerously wrong Jesus had got it all!

Similarly, however merciful and peaceable the prophet Mohammed may have been, his followers now issue fatwas such as that by Nasir al-Fahd: 'If Muslims cannot defeat the *kafir* (unbeliever) in a different way, it is permissible to use any weapons of mass destruction. Even if it kills them all and wipes them and their descendants off the face of the Earth.' Thus monotheism is traduced by its own practitioners in their pursuit of super-natural illusions; religion becomes a tool of power that divides humanity into 'us' and 'them'. This also is a relic of a past we now move beyond. In reality there is simply a mono-anthropy; we live as I and Thou in the present moment.

In a way we have now come full circle to where, as a species, we started – staring from our caves into the vast infinity with fear. As we watch the 'Earthrise' from satellites over the moon we see a fragile blue sphere hovering in the black emptiness of space, mysterious beyond all expectation and comprehension. This is our home. This is all we have, so fragile, alone in the vast infinity; a thin membrane of life enfolding a solitary globe. This realisation brings a new fear: the world that was once despised in favour of the 'super'-natural is now being destroyed in the pursuit of illusory natural ambitions.[8] But now we know that our survival or destruction will be of our own making, our own '*response*-ibility'.

---

7. R. Moore, *The War on Heresy: Faith and Power in Medieval Europe* (Profile Books, 2012).
8. J. Lovelock, *The Revenge of Gaia* (Allan Lane, 2006).

We cannot reconfigure the past nor apprehend the future, all we can do is respond to the present moment. It is here we will find our fulfilment, our destiny. And in the end the most important question for each is simple: what is a good life? As I began with a reference to the death camps I end with the testimony by a family friend, a painter of great talent and a medical doctor – Hans Lochmann – who died an early death after the war from his experiences under the Nazi regime in Germany. His was an unfinished life, but one which was sufficient. As he wrote in his last testament to an aunt, which she subsequently translated:

> One thing I now thoroughly understand – that of all the things in this world one alone is important – that is to say love. Love to whose realisation we must contribute something of ourselves – a comfort, a pleasure or some other thing, the love of a speck of colour, an unessential part of a picture, or that we allow a flower to remain standing instead of pulling it to pieces, or that we gladly do something that costs us to overcome. All this is not new nor original, but how difficult we find it all the same to go on living. How much more difficult to die! For a good death is indeed to be found in this: that we submit what to us appears of endless importance – our Self – which is restless, full of confidence, to a great unknown Mercy.